Fruit & Vegetable

JUICE THERAPY

—Curative and healing powers of fruit and vegetables in ensuring a healthy body & glowing skin!

Dr. Syed Aziz Ahmad
Dr. S.C. Sharma

PUSTAK MAHAL®
Delhi • Bangalore • Mumbai • Patna • Hyderabad • London

J-3/16 , Daryaganj, New Delhi-110002
☎ 23276539, 23272783, 23272784 • *Fax:* 011-23260518
E-mail: info@pustakmahal.com • *Website:* www.pustakmahal.com

Sales Centre

- 10-B, Netaji Subhash Marg, Daryaganj, New Delhi-110002
  ☎ 23268292, 23268293, 23279900 • *Fax:* 011-23280567
  E-mail: rapidexdelhi@indiatimes.com
- **Hind Pustak Bhawan**
  6686, Khari Baoli, Delhi-110006
  ☎ 23944314, 23911979

Branches

Bengaluru: ☎ 080-22234025 • *Telefax:* 080-22240209
E-mail: pustak@airtelmail.in • pustak@sancharnet.in
Mumbai: ☎ 022-22010941, 022-22053387
E-mail: rapidex@bom5.vsnl.net.in
Patna: ☎ 0612-3294193 • *Telefax:* 0612-2302719
E-mail: rapidexptn@rediffmail.com
Hyderabad: *Telefax:* 040-24737290
E-mail: pustakmahalhyd@yahoo.co.in

ISBN 978-81-223-0734-4

Edition : 2012

Printed at : Sharma Printers, Delhi

Dedicated

to

Ammi

—Dr. Syed Aziz Ahmed

Acknowledgement

We are thankful to:

1. The President and Principal of the G.F. (P.G.) College, Shahjahanpur (U.P.) for library and research facilities.
2. Mr. Suresh Chandra Sharma, Incharge—Fruit and Vegetable Preservation Centre, Shahjahanpur (U.P.), Prof. M.S. Usmani and Prof. S. Maudood Ashraf for their suggestions and discussions, and Mr. R.C. Sharma for typing the manuscript.

Contents

Preface

"You're what you savour."— this proverbial maxim forms the basis of 'Phytotherapy' or treatment with fruit and vegetable extracts. The modern nutrition gurus and dieticians call these extracts as 'Nutriceuticals'—an umbrella term for dietary supplements. These are foods, as if especially created by nature for people with specific diseases. Besides providing alternative herbal cures, these act as health tonics to supply vim, vigour and vitality.

The palliative and potent curative aspects of plant products being natural in origin cause no side effects. Instead, these products act as therapeutic or prophylactic medicines. Current Ayurvedic researches by leading pharmaceutical R&D centres around the world have proved their indomitable power to cure or prevent a large number of diseases viz., arthritis, high-cholesterol, hypertension, osteoporosis, diabetes, asthma, and more. The attention of the readers may be drawn to a latest finding by the Ajanta Pharmacy, which has developed the world's first natural 'Carotene' product derived from carrot extract that has proved highly effective in controlling diabetes and obesity.

Fruit & Vegetable Juice Therapy
(A Natural Way to Good Health)

The theme of this book is in line with the thinking of Dr. Adlof, who says "Fruits alone contain healing draughts for man." Nature offers them readymade. They are sure to cure the diseases and ailments because fruits contain nectar (a sugary fluid like honey) and ambrosia (a highly nutritive aromatic food material).

Treatment with fruits is age old. An old saying "An apple a day keeps the doctor away" still holds good as eating an apple a day is good for the lungs, researchers have discovered. A team from St. George's Hospital Medical School, London, studied the diets and lung function of more than 2500 men aged between 45 and 49. The researchers measured the ability to breathe out sharply using a special test called as FEVI. They found that good lung function was associated with high intake of vitamin C, E and beta-carotene, citrus fruits, apples, and fruit juices. But after they took into consideration factors such as body mass, smoking history and exercise, the only food that seemed to make a significant difference was APPLE. It was found that eating five or more apples a week was linked to better lung function. Those who ate apples had a lung capacity higher than who did not.

Vegetable is not far behind as far as nutrition and curative properties are concerned. They are also packed with nutrients but the dark, bright-coloured ones seem to pack the most. One is advised to eat coloured vegetables and fruits so as to get a number of vitamins, minerals and trace elements like copper, zinc, selenium etc. They protect us from a number of diseases. To derive maximum benefit, vegetables should be used fresh in raw form or in the form of juices of single or two-three vegetables.

There are three principal components of food–protein, fat and carbohydrate. All three can be used as fuel (energy) for growth and maintenance of the body.

Protein and carbohydrate supply the almost same amount of energy i.e. 4 calories/gram. Fat provides 9.3 calories/gram. Fat and carbohydrate can be freely consumed, but a good deal of protein in the diet must be conserved as building material.

Besides three basic components, essential substances that cannot be synthesised in the body have to be supplied readymade. These are: vitamins (A, C, B-Complex—water soluble, and D, K, E—fat soluble) and minerals (Cu, Zn, Fe, Mn, Mg, Ca, Se).

A balanced diet constitutes all the above substances in the right proportions: protein, carbohydrate, fat, vitamins and minerals.

Malnutrition which happens mostly in children arises due to inadequate and unbalanced diet. Most of the children die as they do not get proper food and become victims of fatal infections of lungs, intestine, atrophy etc. Even TB, a common curable disease among adults, becomes a serious problem due to inadequate diet.

Malnutrition affects productivity, life expectancy that is the cause of low productivity, thereby adversely affecting the country's economic development. This was stressed at a workshop organised by the Food and Nutrition Board of the Department of Women and Child Development. A recent survey has estimated that loss of productivity due to malnutrition in India is around Rs. 33,000 crore every year. The workshop stressed that awareness in this area would help arrest malnutrition, especially among women and children.

What can we do to overcome Malnutrition

- Nutrition advocacy, sensitisation, capacity building and awareness generation, especially at the grassroot level.
- Preventing onset of malnutrition among 0-2 year old children by promoting complementary feeding of infants at six months, using home-based foods.
- Preventing low birth weight of the new-borns and breaking the inter-generation cycle of malnutrition by addressing

the nutritional needs of the girl child, adolescent girls, pregnant and lactating women.

- Preventing calorie and micro-nutrient malnutrition by promoting community based production of low-cost nutritious foods and consumption of fruits and vegetables.
- Involvement of women's groups in advocating and practising proper nutritional practices.
- People are quite unaware of the nutritive value of fruits and vegetables and always opt for conventional food sources to tackle the problem of malnutrition. But fruits and their juices and other preparations available in the market do not let any child/adult to fall victim of deficiency diseases, if eaten regularly.

●●●

Importance of Fruits and their Natural Benefits

Fruit is an excellent food and medicine as well. Fruits and vegetables may cure serious diseases, especially stomach ailments. By eating fruits one can keep illness at bay. Besides, these are nature's boon for good health and vitality. They have good taste and possess several vitamins and minerals. They act as scavengers in our body and drive away toxins from it. Fruits contain pure water, sugar, vitamins, minerals, alkali, organic acids, proteins, fat, fibre and some aromatic compounds which give sweet smell to them.

Fruits contain 5-15% sugar which is absorbed cent per cent by our body. Fruit's carbohydrate changes into sugar with the help of sunlight. This type of sugar does not need intestinal juice for digestion. So, by eating fruits we take the already digested sugar.

Fruits are alkaline in nature. They decrease the acidity of blood, thereby reducing the workload of lungs, liver and kidney etc. This is the reason why fruits are very useful for **asthma, chronic cold, bronchitis, pleuricy, jaundice** and **kidney** diseases. Ascorbic acid and alkali present in fruits kill the bacteria.

Since fruits contain less protein and fat, so their digestion period in stomach is of shorter duration as compared to other foods. Fruit skin contains much fibre which helps clean the stomach. So, don't peel the skin off the fruits, rather eat them after washing. If the fruit skin is very thick, then scrape it from inside and eat because concentration of vitamins & minerals is quite high just below the fruit skin.

Always drink fresh fruit juice, otherwise it will become sour or stale. Take juice in its natural form i.e. without adding spices or salt. Do not eat fruits in excess as it sometimes causes indigestion. Always eat ilaichi with banana and drink milk after mango. Fruits are much better than cereals. Use them daily after meals.

In the following diseases, fruits provide great relief: **Constipation** (apple, orange, guava, papaya, mosambi); **Acidity** (apple, mosambi, orange, watermelon, carrot); **Gas** (apple, papaya, lemon); **Ulcer** (carrot, narial ka pani); **Piles** (anar, papaya, bael); **Diabetes** (carrot, amla, jamun); **Jaundice** (anar, apple, orange, mosambi, grapes); **Diarrhoea** (anannas, apple, anar); **Cold** (anar, anannas, mosambi, orange, carrot); **Skin disease** (apple, carrot, watermelon, lemon); **Fever** (anar, orange, mosambi); **High B.P.** (anar, papaya, orange, lemon); **Low B.P.** (mosambi, carrot); **Heart disease** (anar, apple, grapes, nashpati, papaya, anannas, lemon).

●●●

Hydrating Effects of Fruits

Water accounts for about 60% of a man's body weight and 50% of a woman's. The difference is because an average woman has a larger proportion of fat, which contains no water. Eating food, especially fruits/vegetables, replaces some of the lost water. All food contains water. The body loses 1.5 litres of water daily. An average diet along with fruit/vegetable may provide 600 ml of free water and the remaining 600-800 ml must be drunk. The kidney must form at least 600 ml of urine to get rid of poisonous matter. About 500 ml water evaporates from the skin, 300 ml from lungs and 100 ml from faeces.

Most of the fruits and vegetables contain 70% water and some fruits contain more as they are quite juicy e.g. citrus fruits, mango, coconut etc. Fruit juices are quite popular now and there is no doubt as far as their natural nutritive value and hydrating effect are concerned. Fruit juices are very common and being sold in the market as health drinks. So, in case of dehydration, they are as valuable as ORS (a solution of sugar—nine spoons, and common salt—one spoon in one litre water).

The National Botanical Research Institute, Lucknow (UP) is going to make herbal drinks available in a variety of blends. Apart from providing instant energy, quenching thirst, fighting fatigue, some of these blends would also give you slight kick as they will have "self-generated alcohol." The drink will be purely natural/herbal, without synthetic preservatives or colours. The blends will be seasonal (for instance, the drinks for the summers will have raw mango pulp as the base ingredient). And to cater to various age groups and needs, the blends will be variegated: the ones for children will be different from those for the elderly persons or pregnant women.

Aerated drinks lack diuretic properties and therefore lead to kidney and gall bladder problems. So, the blends will have barley water and some other diuretic as one of the ingredients. Similarly, the diets of most people these days lack anti-oxidants that protect us from radiation and also neutralises free radicals. Free radicals are known to trigger or promote diseases like cancer. So these drinks are packed with anti-oxidants also.

●●●

FRUITS

– Their Nutritive Value, Preservation & Medicinal Use

Almond (Badam)

Botanical Name : *Prunus amygadalus*
Family Name : Rosaceae
Hindi Name : Badam
Sanskrit Name : Badama
English Name : Almond

Description

Almond is a valuable food remedy for various common diseases. We have bitter and sweet almonds. Avoid using bitter one as it has poison prussic acid. Skin-wise, almonds are of two types — one is hard and the other having thin skin is called *kagzi badam,* which is a better quality.

Distribution

Native of Morocco, in cultivation from ancient times in Syria & Palestine, now cultivated in most of the countries. In India, almond is cultivated in Punjab, Kashmir, Himachal Pradesh.

Part Used

Seed.

Properties

Demulcent, stimulative, nervine, tonic, aphrodisiac.

Forms of Use

Whole seed and oil.

Food Value

The best way of using almonds is to soak them overnight in water, then skin is peeled off and a paste is made, called almond butter. It is now easily digestible and is very nutritious. (250g of almond is equal to 1 kg of milk).

Almond's analysis shows the presence of nutrients in following proportions: (per 100g.)

Moisture	5.2%
Protein	20.8%
Fat	58.9%
Minerals	2.9%
Fibre	1.7%
Carbohydrate	10.5%
Calcium	250 mg
Phosphorus	490 mg
Iron	4.5 mg
Niacin	4.4 mg
B-Complex	Small Amount
Calorific Value	665

Medicinal Uses

(i) The fat in almond consists of the most beneficial unsaturated fatty acids. It lowers serum cholesterol levels.

(ii) It contains copper, iron, phosphorus and vitamin B_1, thus good for health.

(iii) It also corrects biological functions of brain, nerves, bones, heart and liver.

(iv) Its regular use prevents early appearance of wrinkles, dryness of skin, pimples and keeps the face fresh.

(v) As it contains copper and iron, it helps in synthesising blood haemoglobin, thus blood forming.

(vi) It is a potent aphrodisiac. Its regular use increases sexual power.

(vii) It is also very useful in respiratory disorders, cold and cough. A paste of almond with black pepper gives resistance against respiratory problems.

(viii) Almonds soaked in honey overnight, taken in the morning gives strong and healthy constitution (body).

(ix) Almonds oil is a boon for health as it increases brain power, removes constipation, corrects liver & spleen.

(x) Oil of bitter almond is a good remedy for skin diseases.

Apple (Saeb)

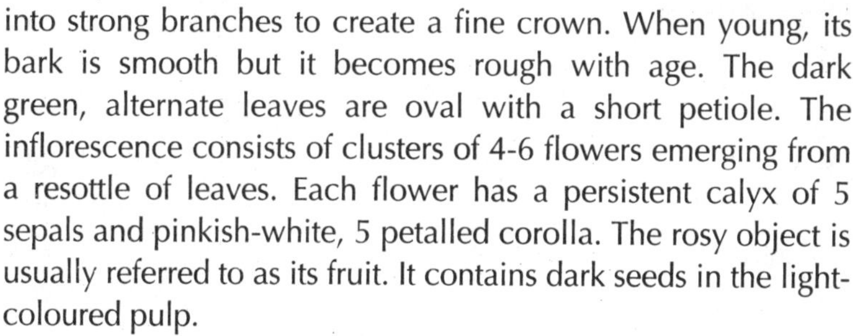

Botanical Name : *Malus sylvestris,* Mill

Family Name : Rosaceae

Hindi Name : Saeb

Sanskrit Name : Sevi

English Name : Apple

Description

Apple tree is rather small. It has a sturdy, erect trunk, that divides into strong branches to create a fine crown. When young, its bark is smooth but it becomes rough with age. The dark green, alternate leaves are oval with a short petiole. The inflorescence consists of clusters of 4-6 flowers emerging from a resottle of leaves. Each flower has a persistent calyx of 5 sepals and pinkish-white, 5 petalled corolla. The rosy object is usually referred to as its fruit. It contains dark seeds in the light-coloured pulp.

Distribution

Apples are cultivated in most of India's hilly regions over an estimated area of 40,000 acres. The important parts where apple is mostly grown are Kashmir, Jammu, Srinagar, Nainital, Almora, Shimla etc.

The types cultivated in India have been mostly introduced from the U.K. and other European countries and the U.S.A.; a few varieties have also been introduced from Australia.

Part Used

Fruit.

Properties

Antacid, nutritive, tranquillizer, anti-uricaemic, anti-diarrhoeic, cardiotonic.

Forms of Use

Fruit, juice, infusion.

Food Value

Apples are valued mainly as dessert fruits. Some types, particularly those with high acid content, are used for culinary purposes. Apples may be preserved for later use after slicing and drying them. They are also canned and jams and jellies are made from them. The juice extracted from apple is used fresh or after fermentation into cider, wine and vinegar. Apple brandy is obtained after distilling the cider.

Apple's analysis shows the presence of nutrients in the following proportions:

Moisture	70%
Protein	0.2%
Fat	0.5%
Fibre	1.0%
Carbohydrate	13.4%
Calcium	10 mg
Phosphorus	14 mg
Iron	1.1 mg
Vitamin B_1	0.12 mg
Vitamin B_2	0.03 mg
Niacin	0.2 mg
Vitamin C	2/100g
Potassium	111 mg
Sodium	2 mg
Chlorine	4 mg
Sulphur	5 mg
Copper	85 mg/100g
Invert Sugar	9.5–17.4
Glucose	2.5–5.6
Fructose	6.5–11.8
Sucrose	1.5–6.0

Malic Acid	0.3–1.0
Tannin	0.02–0.15%
Calorific Value	59

Sugar constitutes 80% of the total carbohydrates of ripe apple. Fructose (60%) is the principal sugar component followed by glucose 25% and sucrose 15%.

Malic acid is the principal acid—90-95% of the total acid in an apple. Citric, lactic and succinic acids are also present barring other acids in traces.

Products/Preservation

Dried Apples & Apple Powder

Dehydrated apples, apple flour or powder find use in bakeries. Apple flour is also used in the treatment of certain types of infant diarrhoea. Vacuum shelf driers are used to obtain a product of superior quality.

Canned & Frozen Apple

Canned apples are usually available in large packings and are used in pies. Apple segments are preserved by dehydro freezing which involves partial drying of prepared fruit to 50% moisture and freezing.

Apple Juice

It is the favoured by-product of apple. Ripe and sound fruits are pressed out in basket-press. The juice thus obtained is strained through a thin cotton cloth and bottled after pasteurization. Fresh apple juice is an amber coloured fluid with mild, delicate flavour.

Murabba

Apple murabba is one of the most popular preparations and is being still used by the people. It is a cardiotonic and controls palpitation. It is prepared by slicing apple, adding equal amount of sugar, citric acid and potassium metabisulphite.

Apple brandy, apple cider, apple butter, apple pomace are the other by-products.

Medicinal Uses

(i) Apples are considered valuable as anti-scorbutic fruits.

(ii) They are rich in pectin and are useful in diarrhoea.

(iii) Apple juice, syrup and vinegar reduce curd tension of milk used in infant feeding.

(iv) Apple murabba, a preserve popular in India, is regarded as a stimulant for heart. It is reported to relieve physical heaviness & mental strain.

(v) It is a natural source of colloidal iron that does not cause diarrhoea, so it suits all kinds of people deficient in iron.

(vi) It cures anaemia synergically.

(vii) An apple a day keeps the doctor away is an old saying, which is still true.

Apricot (Khubani)

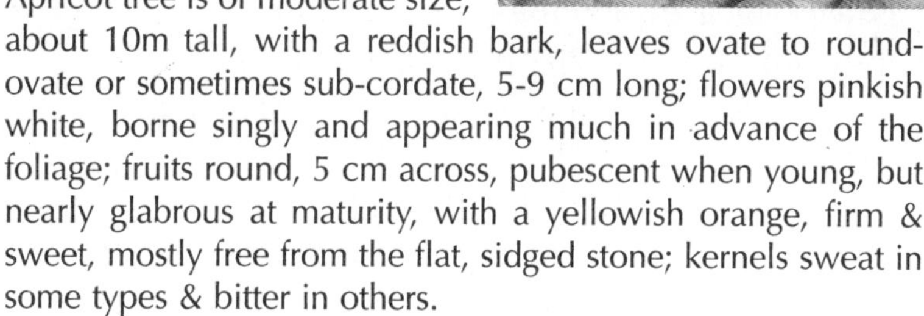

Botanical Name : *Prunus armeniaca*

Family Name : Rosaceae

Sanskrit Name : Hari

Hindi Name : Zardalu/ Khubani

English Name : Apricot

Description

Apricot tree is of moderate size, about 10m tall, with a reddish bark, leaves ovate to round-ovate or sometimes sub-cordate, 5-9 cm long; flowers pinkish white, borne singly and appearing much in advance of the foliage; fruits round, 5 cm across, pubescent when young, but nearly glabrous at maturity, with a yellowish orange, firm & sweet, mostly free from the flat, sidged stone; kernels sweat in some types & bitter in others.

Distribution

The apricot is said to be a native of China and has spread to India, Iran, Egypt & Greece. It is abundant in Himachal Pradesh, Kashmir, Kullu and Shimla hills ascending up to 3000 m.

Parts Used

Fruits.

Properties

Cooling, laxative, refrigerant.

Forms of Use

Fruit as such is eaten.

Food Value

Apricot is used as a table fruit in the regions where it is grown and otherwise also.

Apricot is a good source of sugars and vitamin A, and contains appreciable amounts of thiamine and iron. Fresh Indian apricots yield 86% of edible matter. Analysis of apricot shows the presence of nutrients in following proportions: (per 100 gms.)

Moisture	85.3%
Protein	1.6%
Fat	0.7%
Fibre	2.1%
Carbohydrate	73.4%
Mineral matter	0.7%
Calorific value	306/100 g
Calcium	110 mg
Phosphorus	70 mg
Iron	4.6 mg
Beta-carotene	58 mg
B_1	0.22 mg
B_2	0.13 mg
Nicotitric acid	0.6 mg
Vitamin C	6 mg/100 g

Ripe apricot pulp contains: total solids, 12.4-16.7; insoluble solids, 2.1-3.1; acids (as malic acid), 0.7-2.2; total sugars (as invert sugar), 3.6-8.6; glucose, 3.2-4.8; fructose, 1.4-4.2; sucrose, 1.4-5.4.

Malic acid and citric acid are said to be the principal acids. Presence of tartaric acid and succinic acid is also reported. The free amino acids, identified in apricot are: asparatio, glutamic, threonine, serine, proline, alanina, glycine, valine, leucine, histidine, tyrosina, orginina etc.

Products/Preservation

A number of food products are prepared from apricot as it is a good source of calcium, phosphorus and iron. It is highly perishable and is preserved for use in a number of ways e.g. apricots are canned & dried. They are also frozen, candied or made into paste. In India, small quantities of apricot are processed in U.P. Apricot pulp is cooked and thinly spread on cloth and then rolled and dried, and in this form is said to constitute an important food. In Himachal Pradesh, a number of products are produced from apricot like apricot jam, apricot nectar and apricot papad. In preparation of papad, the fruit is made into pulp which is then dehydrated and pressed. Apricot nectar, a popular beverage, is prepared by steaming and converting the ripe soft fruit into purce and mixing it with sugar syrup containing some citric acid. Apricot beverages have low acidity and therefore tend to be somewhat flat; they blend particularly well with more acid fruit juices, such as orange or pineapple. Apricot leather is extensively used in drinks and sauces after treatment with sulphur dioxide as preservative and mixing the same with sucrose (5%) and glucose syrup (5%). The golden coloured product is highly nutritious and has a vitamin A potency of 7000 I.U./100g.

Medicinal Uses

(i) Apricot kernel oil is used for food purposes and in cosmetic and pharmaceutical preparations.

(ii) It also finds use in medicine for different ailments.

(iii) It is advised to persons suffering from fever as it has cooling effect.

(iv) It is also useful as laxative.

(v) Its juice is very refreshing.

Banana (Kela)

Botanical Name : *Musa paradisiaca,* Linn

Family Name : Musaceae

Hindi Name : Kela

Sanskrit Name : Kadali

English Name : Banana, Plantain

Description

Musa, the biggest and geographically the most widespread, includes the majority of edible bananas, mostly of hybrid origin. Edible bananas of hybrid origin valued for their seedless fruits are included under this specific name. They comprise all the diploid, triploid or tetraploid clones, mainly hybrids of M. acuminata and M. balbisiana.

Distribution

A genus of perennial tree-like herbs, Musa is widely distributed in moist tropics, from Africa in the west to the Polynesian Island in the east. About 14 species have been recorded in India; 3 or 4 exotic species are cultivated for ornament. Most of the cultivated or commercially important bananas particularly those occurring in India belong to Musa genus.

Parts Used

Fruit, flowers, stem, root & leaves.

Properties

Aromatic, cooling, anti-ulcer, diuretic, stimulant, antidysentric, hypoglycemic, anthelmintic.

Form of Use

Fruit pulp, juice of full ripe banana, unripe banana, banana powder and boiled unripe banana as vegetable.

Food Value

Banana is one of the most important fruit and vegetable crops of India. Not only it is cultivated on a large scale as a field crop but it is also widely grown as a backyard crop in the households. In certain parts of Kerala, in many Pacific Islands and in tropical Africa, banana forms a staple food of the people. Fresh fruit is eaten as dessert, while unripe fruit and cooking-type varieties are eaten as vegetable. Fruit pulp is dried and processed into flour or preserved in many forms for subsequent use. Fruits are used in various Indian confections like *rasayanam* and *panchamrutam,* sugar coated chips, toffee, coffee substitutes, jams and jellies. It is also canned.

The ripe fruit is a rich source of carbohydrates and a fair source of minerals & vitamins, particularly B-complex.

Banana's analysis shows the presence of nutrients in the following proportions (per 100 gms):

Contents	**Unripe banana**	**Ripe banana**
Moisture	60-72%	60-79%
Protein	1.0-1.8%	0.4-1.7%
Reducing sugar	0.1-02%	3.6-24.6%
Non-reducing sugar	0.5%	14.6%
Fat	24.5%	16.4%
Ash	0.9-1.36%	0.7-1.6%
Calories	-	116 cal/100 g
Starch	20.5%	-
Sodium	67/100 g	34.8/100 g
Potassium	382 mg	401 mg
Calcium	10 mg	9 mg
Magnesium	-	28 mg
Manganese	-	0.8 mg
Copper	-	0.2 mg
Iron	0.6 mg	0.6 mg
Phosphorus	30 mg	31 mg
Sulphur	-	10.0 mg
Chlorine	-	125 mg
Silica	-	23.8 mg
Iodine	-	Minute Quantity

Aluminium	-	Minute Quantity
Zinc	-	Minute Quantity
Cobalt	-	Minute Quantity
Arsenic	-	Minute Quantity

The main principal sugars present in ripe banana are sucrose, glucose, fructose, and maltose. Amino acids present in ripe banana are: arginine, histidine, isoleucine, leucine, lysine, methronine, phenylalamine, threonine, tryptophan and valine.

As far as vitamins are concerned, their values in ripe banana are as follows: β-carotene (as Vit. A), 8-470 I.U., thiamine (Vit. B_1), 20-51 μg; riboflavin (Vit. B_2), 21-71 μg; niacin, 0.5-0.8 mg; ascorbic acid (Vit. C), 5-17mg/100 g; pantothenic acid, pyridoxin (Vit. B_6), biotin (Vit. H), inositol, folic acid and tocopherol (Vit. E) present in minute quantity.

The aroma and flavour characteristic of banana develop during ripening. Amyl acetate is the main odorous constituent besides amyl butyrate, acetaldelyde, ethyl and methyl alcohols.

Malic acid is the main principal acid present in the ripe banana; citric and oxalic acids are also present. It also contains a number of enzymes (e.g. amylase, in vertase etc.)

Banana Products

(a) ***Chips*** – Fully mature but unripe banana is cut into chips like potato and consumed after frying in oil.

(b) ***Flour and Powder*** – Banana flour is prepared from unripe fruits, and banana powder from ripe fruits. The former is essentially starchy, while the latter is rich in sugars. For the preparation of flour, dried banana chips are powdered in a mill and sifted through sieves. Analysis of banana flour shows the following nutrient composition: moisture 10.2-10.9; carbohydrate 79.6-83.3; protein 2.8-4.9; fibre 0.7-1.4; ash 2.0-3.0%. It is used to prepare infant food.

Banana powder is prepared from the pulp of ripe fruits which is mashed and dried in drum or spray driers. The dried product is pulverized and passed through a 20 mesh sieve. Analysis: total sugar 68.8%; starch 7.2%; protein 5.0%; fibre 1.5%; pectin 2.5%; citric acid 2.2%;

and ash 3.17%. Banana powder may also be used in the preparation of various food items.

(c) ***Banana Fig*** – Banana fig is the popular name for dried ripe fruits. For making figs, peeled fruits are split longitudinally, each half cut into pieces about one inch in length and dried in the sun till pliable and soft. Figs keep well for 3-4 months. A product with attractive appearance and good keeping quality is obtained by dipping banana pieces for 15 minutes in sodium carbonate solution (1%) followed by washing in water, exposure to "SO_2" fumes for an hour and drying in oven at 55-60°. It is used for making puddings.

Medicinal Uses

(i) Bananas contain two physiologically important compounds: Serotenin and nor-epinephrine, in addition to dopamine, 3, 4-dihydroxy phenyl alanine and an unidentified compound catecholamine. The concentration of some of the compounds in the pulp and peel of ripe banana found to be as follows: pulp—serotenin-8-50 mg/g; nor-epinephrine-1.9 mg/g; and dopamine-7.9 μ/g; peel—serotenin-47-93 μg/g; nor-epinephrine-122 μg/g and dopamine-700 μg/g. Serotenin inhibits gastric secretion and stimulates smooth muscle in the intestine and elsewhere; nor-epinephrine is a mediator of autonomic function and is widely used as a vasoconstrictor agent. Serotenin is apparently well tolerated when administered orally to human beings; doses up to 20 mg of serotenin cause no adverse effect. The therapeutic uses of banana (in colon disease, constipation, peptic ulcer, etc.) may be due to the presence of these active principles.

(ii) Banana fruit has mild laxative properties that help to ease constipation.

(iii) The fruit aids in combating diarrhoea and dysentery and promotes the healing of intestinal lesions in ulcerative colitis.

(iv) Banana powder is effective in the treatment of colon disease, sprue and other forms of carbohydrate intolerance in children; it is also used for certain intestinal disorders in adults.

(v) It forms a useful constituent of the diet of infants; a syrup prepared of the ripe fruit may be incorporated with milk and used for infant feeding.

(vi) The ripe fruit is reported to be useful in diabetes, uremia, nephritis, gout, hypertension and cardiac diseases.

(vii) Unripe fruit and cooked flowers are useful in diabetes.

(viii) Vegetable prepared from unripe banana helps in healing the intestinal ulcer.

(ix) The juice of flowers is used for dysentery and stem and root for disorders of the blood.

(x) Ripe banana is useful in acidity. Heartburn resulting from tea consumption may be neutralized by taking two ripe bananas just before taking tea.

(xi) The banana plant juice is astringent; it quenches thirst in cholera; it is also given in nervous disorders like hysteria, epilepsy etc.

(xii) Ripe banana is aphrodisiac, demulcent and aperient.

(xiii) The fruit is eaten to relieve soreness of the throat and chest accompanied with dry cough; it is also given in irritability of the bladder; the ripe fruit is a laxative.

(xiv) The ash of the banana skin is used for dressing wounds.

(xv) An ounce of the ripe fruit mixed with a little tamarind and salt is a household remedy for diarrhoea & dysentery.

(xvi) Banana is said to promote regeneration of red blood cells and to stimulate haemoglobin production.

(xvii) It is a useful constituent of various nourishing foods for infants.

Black Berry (Jamun)

Botanical Name	: *Syzygium cuminii*
Family Name	: Myrtaceae
Hindi Name	: Jamun
Sanskrit Name	: Jambu
English Name	: Black Berry

Description

About 75 species of black berry are found in India. A genus of trees or shrubs, it is distributed in the tropics. Some species bear edible fruits, a few yield timber and some species give the cloves of commerce.

Black Berry tree is a large and evergreen tree with leaves opposite, 8-20 cm long, leathery. Fruit 1.5-4 cm long, violet black when ripe. Seed usually one. Fruit is eaten raw [illegible] salt. It makes the tongue purplish for hours.

Distribution

Grown throughout the plains of India.

Parts Used

Fruit, leaves, seed & bark.

Properties

Stomachic, astringent, diuretic, antidiabetic.

Forms of Use

Fruit, juice, vinegar, seed powder.

Food Value

The ripe fruit is widely eaten in India. The edible pulp forms 75% of the whole fruit. Analysis of the edible part shows the following composition (per 100 gms):

Moisture	83.7%
Protein	0.7%

Fat	0.3%
Fibre	0.9%
Carbohydrate	14.0%
Ash	0.4%
Calcium	15 mg
Phosphorus	15 mg
Magnesium	35 mg
Iron	1.2 mg
Vitamin A	80 I.U.
Vitamin B_1	0.03 mg
Vitamin B_2	0.01 mg
Neotinic acid	0.2 mg
Vitamin C	18 mg
Choline	7 mg
Folic acid	3 mg

Glucose and fructose are the principal sugars in ripe fruit; not even a trace of cane sugar is found. Malic acid is the major acid (0.5% of the wt. of fruit); a small quantity of oxalic acid is also reported. Gallic acid and tannins account for the astringency of the fruit.

The purple colour of the fruit is due to the presence of flavours and anthocyanin pigments occurring as plant diglycosides.

Products/Preservation

Purple fruit is liked by all and eaten throughout India. A wine is prepared from ripe fruit in Goa. It is used for making squashes and jellies. A good jelly can be made from the purple-fleshed fruits. A jam can also be prepared from pitted fruits. The juice of unripe fruits is used for preparing vinegar.

Medicinal Uses

(i) Juice of ripe fruit made into vinegar is used as stomadic, carminative and diuretic.

(ii) Ripe fruit is eaten to combat diabetes.

(iii) Fruits and seeds are hypoglycemic agents.

(iv) A single dose of extract of seeds produces 15 to 25% fall in fasting blood sugar in 4 to 5 hours after taking it orally.

(v) It is a powerful anti-diarrhoeic agent, and controls diarrhoea gradually.

(vi) Ripe fruit juice is used in the enlargement of spleen and suppressed or scanty urine.

(vii) Leaf juice is a useful remedy for dysentery with blood (one spoon juice three/four times daily).

Custard Apple (Sharifa)

Botanical Name : *Annona squamosa,* Linn

Family Name : Annonaceae

Hindi Name : Sharifa

Sanskrit Name : Sitaphal

English Name : Custard apple

Description

Custard apple is a large genus, comprising over 70 species of trees and shrubs, distributed in tropical countries. Its five or six species, some of which yield edible fruits, have been introduced in India.

Its tree is small, more or less evergreen, 15-20 ft. high, bearing yellowish green fruit 3-4" in diameter. The flesh of the fruit is juicy, cream yellow or white, delicately flavoured, and tastes sweet. The seeds are mainly brownish-black smooth and oblong.

Distribution

This tree occurs wild and is also cultivated all over India.

Parts Used

Leaves, bark, root, seed & fruit.

Properties

Astringent, tonic, anthelmintic, purgative, diuretic and anti-cancerous.

Forms of Use

Fruit, root powder, decoction.

Food Value

Custard apple has a pleasant flavour. It can be made into drinks, and fermented liquor. The pulp contains:

Moisture	73.2%
Glucose	14.5%
Saccharose	1.7%
Protein	0.8%
Ascorbic acid	50 mg/100g

The unripe fruit, seed, leaf and root are considered medicinal.

Fruit Preservation

Semi-ripe fruits are usually preserved under refrigeration but it is very difficult to preserve over-ripe fruits.

Medicinal Uses

(i) It is found to have anti-cancerous properties against human epidermal cercinoma of the Nasopharynx in tissue culture.

(ii) Ripe fruit bruised and mixed with salt is applied to malignant tumours to hasten suppuration (pus formation) and healing.

(iii) The unripe fruit is useful in destroying insects and lices.

(iv) The fruit seeds are also abortifaciat.

(v) It is considered an anti-scorbutic.

(vi) Fruit seeds were found to have oxytocic and some uterotonic activity.

(vii) Its powdered seeds give a good hair wash.

(viii) Unripe fruits are used in diarrhoea, dysentery and dyspepsia.

(ix) Leaf juice, when applied over head, kills lice.

(x) Leaf juice is also helpful in hysterical or fainting fits when inhaled.

Date (Khajoor)

Botanical Name : *Phoenix dactylifera*
Family Name : Pinaceae
Hindi Name : Khajoor
Sanskrit Name : Kharjoor
English Name : Date

Description

The date tree is tall, up to 36 m in height, cultivated or occasionally found self-sown in some parts of India. Its trunk covered with persistent bases of petioles, the base usually surrounded by a mass of offshoots or suckers; leaves in open crown, pinnate, up to 5 m long, greyish green; pinnae 20-40 cm long, linear, keeled, lower pinnae modified into spines; flowers in branched spadices, small; fruit an oblong berry, 2.5-7.5 cm long reddish or yellowish brown when ripe.

Distribution

Date palm has been known to exist from prehistoric times in the warm dry zones. It is believed to be indigenous to Persian Gulf, Iran being the most important centre of the date production. In India, it is cultivated in Rajasthan, Gujarat and Punjab.

Parts Used

Fruit.

Properties

Nutritive, tonic, demulcent, expectorant, laxative & aphrodisiac.

Forms of Use

Fruit is eaten raw. Dried fruit is also used.

Food Value

Dates are rich in sugars and are eaten fresh or dried. They form an important item of food in the Arabian countries from time immemorial.

Analysis of the edible matter of freshly dried dates (edible matter 86%, seed 14%) gave following results (per 100 gms):

Moisture	15.3%
Protein	2.5%
Fat	0.4%
Carbohydrate	75.8%
Fibre	4%
Mineral matter	2.1%
Phosphorus	0.05 mg
Calcium	0.12 mg
Iron	7.3 mg
B-carotene	44 I.U.
Thiamine (B_1)	0.011 mg
Riboflavin (B_2)	0.023 mg
Nicotinic acid	0.9 mg
Ascorbic acid	3 mg
Calorific Value	317

The mineral composition of dried dates is as follows:

Potassium	754 mg
Calcium	67.9 mg
Magnesium	58.5 mg
Iron	1.61 mg
Copper	0.21 mg
Phosphorus	63.8 mg
Sulphur	51.0 mg/100g

Presence of zinc, arsenic and iodine is also reported.

The main components of ripe dates are sugars (85% of total solids) mainly sucrose & invert sugar (glucose + flucose).

Analysis of the edible portion (80%) of the dried hard preserved dates known as chhuhara gave the following composition:

Moisture	11.9%
Protein	2.9%
Fat	0.5%
Carbohydrate	83%
Ash	1.8%
Calcium	36 mg
Phosphorus	130 mg
Iron	3.5 mg
Calorific Value	347 cal/100 g.

Products/Preservation

Dates are widely used in bakery preserves or added in cakes and in dishes with milk, butter, meat, etc; a type of honey is also prepared from them. Dates can be canned as a paste after pitting, grinding and mixing with invert sugar syrup. Date syrup (invert sugar, 70%) obtained by extracting the fruit hot water and concentrating in vacuum, has a mild sweet taste and may be used in the manufacture of gingerbread.

Medicinal Uses

(i) Dates are demulcent, expectorant and laxative and are used in respiratory diseases and fever.

(ii) They are also reported to be used in cases of memory disturbance.

(iii) Dates are powerful nutritious fruit, useful in anaemia.

(iv) It is aphrodisiac in nature.

(v) Dried dates soaked in milk are highly nutritious and give vitality.

(vi) Date is prescribed in asthma, chest complaint & cough.

(vii) It is also useful in gonorrhoea.

Fig (Anjir)

Botanical Name : *Ficus carica, L. (Common fig)*
Family Name : Moraceae
Hindi Name : Anjir
Sanskrit Name : Anjir
English Name : Fig

Description

Fig grows on a bush or small tree with cylindrical stem. The tree grows to a height of about 15-30 ft. and has ample latex producing ducts. It has broad ovate or nearly orbicular leaves, more or less deeply 3-5 lobed, rough above and pubescent below; fruit, usually pear-shaped, variable in size and colour.

Distribution

The fig plant is considered to be a native of Asia region and is grown nearly in all tropical and sub-tropical countries. It is now cultivated and found all over India.

Parts Used

Bark, leaves, fruit.

Properties

Pectoral, laxative, emollient, energy giving, antiboil, nutritive & tonic.

Forms of Use

Its main use is as an edible nutritive fruit; its secondary uses are as a decoction and as a poultice.

Food Values

Figs are consumed fresh, dried, preserved, candied or canned. Fresh figs are delicious and may be used as dessert or for jam. Bulk of the crop is consumed as dried fruit. Better grades of dried figs are used for making fancy packs, while other grades are used for the production of alcohol and wine.

Fresh fig is a delicious fruit with high nutritive value. It consists of 84% pulp and 16% skin. The chemical composition varies with type. The average composition of the edible part of the fresh Indian fig is as follows (per 100gms):

Moisture	80.8%
Protein	1.3%
Mineral matter	0.6%
Carbohydrates	17.1%
Calcium	0.06 mg
Phosphorus	0.03 mg
Iron	1.2 mg
B-carotene	270 I.U.
Nicotinic acid	0.6 mg
Riboflavin (B_2)	50 µg
Ascorbic acid	2 mg/100 g

Figs owe their food value chiefly to their mineral and sugar contents. The total mineral content is 2 to 4 times that of most other fresh foods. Only cheese and a few nuts have a higher calcium content than fig. It is richer in iron and copper than nearly all fruits. Traces of zinc are also reported to be present. Both fresh and dried figs contain appreciable quantities of vitamin A and C (30% of the Vitamin A activity is lost in drying) and smaller amounts of vitamins of the B-group and other vitamins. A comparison of the nutritive index of fig and other fruits is as follows: fig-11; apple-9; date-6; and pear-6.

The total sugar content of fresh figs is 13-20% and that of dried figs is 42-62%. Sugar is present mostly in the form of invert sugar. Analysis of fresh and dried figs showed presence of 15.2-45-95% of reducing sugars.

The principal acids in fresh figs are citric and acetic. Small amounts of malic, boric and oxalic acids are also present. The acid content ranges from 0.1 to 0.44% (as citric acid). Fresh figs also contain gum and mucilage (0.8%) and pentosons (0.83%). A phosphatide with a nitrogen: phosphorus ratio at 1:2 and containing palmitic and oleic acids is reported to be present.

Analysis of fig skin gave the following composition (per 100 gms):

Moisture	76.3%
Protein	1.5%
Fat	0.5%
Fibre	2.3%
Carbohydrate	18.7%
Ash	0.7%
Calcium	162 mg
Phosphorus	233 mg
Sugar	5.4%
Gum-mucilage	2.74%
Sugar in fig juice	20.7%

Fig seeds contain both unsaturated and saturated fatty acids e.g. oleic acid 18.99; linoleic acid 33.72 and linolenic acid 32.95 (unsaturated); palmitic acid 5.23; stearic acid 2.18% (saturated acids) etc.

The milk clotting activity of fresh fig latex is reported to be 30-100 times rennet prepared from calf stomach mucosa. For preparing the rennet, the latex is collected in the early morning hours when both the yield and the enzyme activity are high. A solid preparation may be obtained from the latex (which contain rennin, proteolytic enzymes, diastase, esterase, lipase, catalase and peroxidase apart from sugar, malic acid etc.) by direct drying in vacuum where a white solid is obtained. One c.c. of the latex yields 0.10 to 0.15 g of the dry powder which retains 90-95% of the activity originally present in the latex for several months at room temperature, more if ascorbic acid is added.

Ficus rennet coagulates milk and also milk-like preparations from vegetable seeds. It may be used for the preparation of cheese and junkets, in other food processing industries and in medicine.

Handling of green unripe figs frequently causes severe erytheme and vesiculation. The principle responsible for this effect is present in the latex and is soluble in aqueous alcohol.

Preservation of Fig

Figs are preserved by drying. Ripened figs are carefully picked and spread in trays in single layers and exposed to moist sulphur fumes for 20-30 minutes. They are exposed to the sun in wooden racks and turned over daily for 5-7 days to ensure even drying. Before the drying is complete, figs are pressed flat to economise packing space and to improve their appearance. Before packing they are dipped in boiling salt solution (3%) to render them soft and to improve the taste. Sun dried figs are graded according to size and colour. First grade figs possess a semi-transparent rosy skin, beautifully streaked at the stalk end; second grade figs are darker and less attractive in appearance.

A novel way of preservation could be to put the properly dried figs into honey. These will be highly nutritious and wholesome.

Sherbet of anjir is also prepared and available in the market to cater to the needs of people suffering from stomach trouble, indigestion, flatulence and dyspepsia.

Medicinal Uses

(i) Fig, fresh or dried, is valued for its laxative property.

(ii) It is diuretic, demulcent, emollient and nutritive.

(iii) It is used in the form of confection and syrups along with senna for constipation.

(iv) Figs are considered useful in the prevention of nutritional anaemias.

(v) The ash of figs is highly alkaline and used in acidity and urinary trouble.

(vi) Fig latex is used as an anthelmintic. The anthelmintic action has been traced to ficin, a proteolytic enzyme which has the remarkable power of digesting living worms. Ficin is effective against both Trichurus and Ascaris. As it gets destroyed by dilute hydrochloric acid, ficin has to be administered simultaneously with sodium carbonate.

(vii) *Sherbet* Anjir or *Ark* Anjir available in the market is used to cure many stomach ailments like dyspepsia, indigestion, flatulence and amoebiasis.

(viii) Fig is high in calories and is easy to digest and assimilate. The latex that oozes out of the freshly cut unripe fruit/leaves contains chymase (a milky fluid with a coagulant action), lipase, amylase and protease. It also contains a diastasic enzyme which when applied over uncooked meat increases maturation process.

(ix) Fig is a highly nutritious fruit. Since it does not contain any fibre, persons recovering from illness are especially advised to take it. It is a wholesome food which is easily digested.

(x) It is also effective in removing gravel from the kidney or bladder and also helps in the removal of the obstruction of the liver and spleen in subacute cases.

(xi) The fruit is also given as a cure for piles & gout.

(xii) It is also liver corrective and used to control diarrhoea.

(xiii) Fig is used in leucoderma or white spots on skin as it contains a chemcial "furo-coumarin" which is responsible for this action. A person suffering from this disease is advised to take figs in any form for 2/3 months.

Gooseberry (Amla)

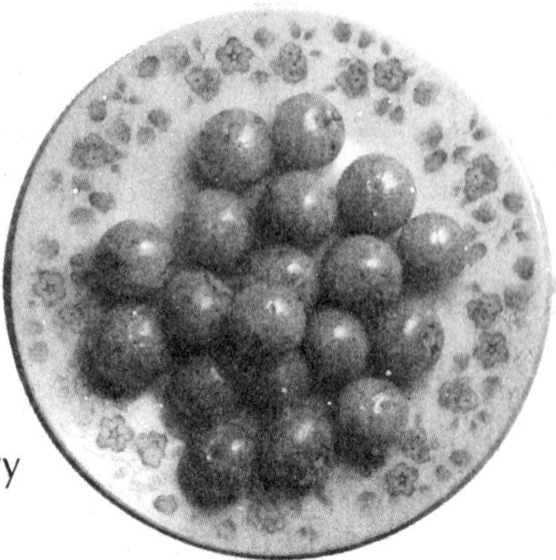

Botanical Name : *Emblica officinalis,* Gaertn

Family Name : Eupho-rbiaceae

Hindi Name : Amla

Sanskrit Name : Adiphala

English Name : Indian gooseberry

Description

Gooseberry is a small genus of tree, native of India, Ceylon, Malaya and China. It is a medium-sized tree with smooth greenish grey bark. Leaves feathery with small narrowing oblong, pinnately arranged leaflets. Fruits globose, ½-1" in diameter, fleshy six lobed containing six trigonous seeds.

Distribution

It is cultivated throughout India, often found in backyard home garden. It is also reported to be found in forests of India ascending up to 4500 ft.

Parts Used

Fruit.

Properties

Astringent, sour, anti-scurvy, cooling, refrigerant, diuretic, anti-dysenteric, stomachic, laxative, hypoglycemic, anti-cancerous.

Forms of Use

Fruit, juice and its jam, jelly & pickles.

Food Value

The fruit is green when tender, changes to light yellow or brick-red colour when matured. It is sour and astringent, and occasionally eaten raw. It is used for making pickles, preserves and jellies. The fruit pulp contains (per 100 gms):

Moisture	81.2%
Protein	0.5%
Fat	0.1%
Fibre	3.4%
Mineral matter	0.7%
Carbohydrate	14.1%
Calcium	0.05 mg
Phosphorus	0.02 mg
Iron	1.2 mg
Calories/K cal	58
Nicotinic acid	1.2 mg
Vitamin C (Pulp)	600 mg/100 g
Vitamin C (Juice)	921 mg/100 g

Small amount of beta-carotene and vitamins B_1 & B_2 also present.

Amla fruit is probably the richest known source of vitamin C. The fruit juice contains nearly 20 times as much vitamin C as orange juice and is single fruit with equal anti-scorbutic value. Feeding trials on healthy human subjects show that the vitamin present in the fruit is utilized as pure ascorbic acid. When administered to patients suffering from pulmonary tuberculosis, Vitamin C saturation is more quickly reached with Amla powder than synthetic vitamin C, thereby showing that the former is more readily assimilated, probably due to the presence of accessory factors or probably going synergic.

Products/Preservation

A tannin containing gallic acid, ellagic acid and glucose in its molecule and naturally present in amla fruit, prevents or retards oxidation of the vitamin and renders the fruit a valuable anti-scorbutic in the fresh as well as in dry condition. The anti-scorbutic value is better retained by preserving the fruits in salt solution or in the form of dry powder. The dried fruit loses only 20% of its vitamin in 375 days when kept in a refrigerator, but loses 67% in the same period when stored at room temperature.

Amla is very much liked in forms of pickles, murabba, jam and jelly. Since it contains ample vitamin C, it does not go stale easily.

Medicinal Uses

Amla fruit has been held in high esteem in indigenous medicine. Its uses are:

(i) The raw fruit is eaten as an aperient.

(ii) Dried fruit is useful in haemorrhage, diarrhoea and dysentery.

(iii) In combination with iron, it is used as a remedy for anaemia, jaundice & dyspepsia.

(iv) A fermented liquor prepared from the fruit is used in jaundice, dyspepsia & cough.

(v) Emblic myrobalan is used in many compound preparations.

(vi) Acute bacillary dysentery may be arrested by drinking a sherbet of amla with lemon juice.

(vii) Triphala, consisting of equal parts of powdered emblic myrobalan, chebulic myrobalan *(Terminalia chebula)* and belleric myrobalan *(Terminalia bellerica)* is used as a laxative and in headache, biliousness, dyspepsia, constipation, piles, enlarged liver and ascites.

(viii) The exudation from incisions on the fruit is used as an external application for inflammation of the eye.

(ix) The dried fruit is detergent and is used as shampoo for the head.

(x) An oil extracted from the fruit is reported to have the property of promoting hair growth.

(xi) The seeds are used in the treatment of asthma, bronchitis and biliousness.

(xii) A preparation from amla fruit called *Jawaris Amla Soda** keeps liver healthy and amoebic dysentry at bay.

---

*An Ayurvedic/Unani preparation

Grape (Angur)

Botanical Name : *Vitis vinifera*
Family Name : Vitiaceae
Hindi Name : Angur
Sanskrit Name : Draksha
English Name : Grape

Description

Grape grows on a climbing shrub that has an erect, somewhat contorted stem with dark brown bark that peels off in strips. The branches have a number of tendrils which enable the plant to cling on to supports. The alternate leaves which are opposite the tendrils and carried on a sturdy petiole, are palmate and 3-5 lobed with a glabrous surface. The flowers are grouped in panicles, each flower having a 5-lobed calyx and a pale green, 5-petalled corolla. The fruit is a berry which varies in colour; in the juicy pulp a few pear shaped seeds (pips) are immersed.

Distribution

Grape is cultivated extensively in most parts of India. However, grapes come to us out of the abyss of antiquity. Their ancient origin is Europe and North America.

Parts Used

Fruit, leaves.

Properties

Astringent, anti-inflammatory, tonic, cooling.

Forms of Use

Decoction, fruit, juice, dry fruit.

Food Value

More than 50 species of *vitis* are known today. Of these, *vitis vinifera* is the most important and is universally cultivated grape-vine. Grape fruit analysis gave following composition (per 100 gms):

Moisture	85.0%
Carbohydrate	16.5%
Protein	0.5%
Fat	0.3%
Fibre	3%
Calorific Value	71
Calcium	20 mg
Phosphorus	30 mg
Iron	0.5 mg
Niacin	0.7 mg
Vitamin C	1 mg/100 g

Small amount of beta-carotene & B-complex also present.

The vitamin content of grapes varies with species. Red or purplish grapes are rich in vitamins as compared to white. The vitamin content increases during maturation, except for biotin (Vit-H) which decreases. The content of thiamine increases three-to-four fold during maturation. There is a loss of vitamins during the processing of grapes for making wine.

Fresh grapes contain varying, but small, quantities of vitamin C and small amount of dehydro-ascorbic acid.

Grapes are good sources of bioflavonoids (Vitamin P) which are known to be useful in such conditions as *purpura, capillary bleeding* in diabetes, oedema and inflammation from injury, radiation damage and atherosclerosis. The berries also contain enzyme invertase etc.

Depending on the type and the locality in which the vine are cultivated, the total sugar content of the ripe grapes generally varies from 9.68 to 18.9% on fresh-weight basis. The major sugars of grapes are glucose and fructose.

The amino acids of grape are arginine, proline, glycine, leucine, phenylalanine, lysine, histidine, isoleucine, valine, methionine and tryptophan.

Grapes contain large amount of tartaric and malic acids. Citric acid is present in small amount. Other acids present are: succinic, fumaric, glyceric, p-coumaric and caffeic acids. It also contains phenolic compounds besides other compounds.

Products/Preservation

(a) ***Wines*** – About 80 per cent of the grapes production is crushed for wine-making.

(b) ***Kishmish*** – Berries of selected types are used for canning where kishmish and munnakka are obtained (both canned products.)

(c) ***Grape-juice*** – Coloured as well as white grapes may be used for making grape-juice. In the case of coloured type, a preliminary heating of the crushed mass at 60-65° for a few minutes is necessary for extracting the colouring matter. The juice is extracted from crushed grapes by means of a basket-press, filtered and set aside for some time to remove cream of tartar. The clear juice is bottled and pasteurised. Grape juice is a very popular product.

Medicinal Uses

(i) Grapes, both fresh and dried, have varied uses in Ayurvedic and Unani systems of medicine. Fresh grapes are considered laxative, stomachic, diuretic, demulcent and cooling.

(ii) Grapes are used in the preparation of various medicinal preparations. The popular tonic *Drashasava* is made from grape juice.

(iii) Grapes are also used in the preparation of *Chavanprash,* a general health tonic.

(iv) The juice of the unripe berries is used as an astringent in throat infections.

(v) Grapes tartar is used in the treatment of constipation.

(vi) Dry grapes–*Munakka*–are used as a popular laxative.

(vii) People with a torpid liver or sluggish biliary function are sometimes advised to undergo a special cure based on eating grapes.

Guava (Amrud)

Botanical Name : *Psidium guajava,* Linn

Family Name : Myrtaceae

Hindi Name : Amrud

Sanskrit Name : Perukam

English Name : Guava

Description

A large genus of tropical and sub-tropical tree and shrubs, Guava is a native of tropical America. Its three species are cultivated in India, the most important of which is *Psidium guava.*

An arborecent shrub or small tree, up to eight metre high; leaves light green, finely pubescent and chartaceous, flowers white and fragrant, fruits green to light yellow, but in some varieties, red, varying in shape and size to a great extent; flesh creamish white yellow, in some verieties red.

Distribution

Guava is often referred to as the apple of the tropics; it is a native of tropical America and has long been naturalized in India. Many varieties are known in cultivation, but a detailed horticultural and systematic study of the species and varieties is still lacking. However, common guava is cultivated throughout India.

Parts Used

Fruit & leaves.

Properties

Fruit is tonic, cooling, laxative, astringent, anti-diarrhoea and anti-dysentric.

Forms of Use

Leaves decoction, ripe fruit, jam & jelly.

Food Value

The guava is a sweet, juicy and highly flavoured fruit, eaten mostly as fresh fruit. It may also be canned, preserved or made into jam, butter, marmalades, pies, ketchups and chutneys. In some countries, guava juice is said to make an excellent substitute for orange or tomato juice in child feeding.

Guava is one of the richest natural sources of vitamin C and contains 4 to 10 times of this vitamin content in citrus fruits. It also contains considerable amount of pectin. As compared to mango and apricot, guava is deficient in vitamin A but superior in most other major nutrients. Analysis of common guava is as follows (100 gms):

Moisture	81.7%
Protein	0.9%
Fat	0.3%
Fibre	5.2%
Carbohydrates	11.2%
Mineral matter	0.7%
Calcium	28 mg
Magnesium	8 mg
Oxalic acid	14 mg
Phosphorus	28 mg
Iron	1.4 mg
Sodium	5.5 mg
Potassium	91 mg
Copper	0.3 mg
Sulphur	14 mg
Chlorine	4 mg
Thiamine (B_1)	0.03 mg
Riboflavin	0.03 mg
Nicotinic acid	0.4 mg
Vitamin C	212/100 g

Vitamin C content of guava shows wide varieties and ranges from 100 to as high as 1000 mg/100 g. It is highest in the fruit skin and in the flesh next to it and decreases in the inner portions of the fruit. Also maximum ascorbic acid oxidase activity is localised in the core of the fruit. The Vitamin C value increases with maturity and reaches its maximum when the fruit is fully mature, but declines when the fruit becomes over-ripe and soft. Some people say that pink-fleshed types are richer in vitamin C than white fleshed ones. Among the important types grown in India (UP), Chittidar has been found to be the richest in Vitamin C value. But the Vitamin C content varies in stages as follows:

Unripe	244.5 mg
Ripe	304.5 mg
Over-ripe	222.5/100 g

Guava is reported to contain a bound form of Vitamin C ascorbigeon, amounting to about 15% of the total Vitamin C content.

Citric is the major acid in guava, tarturic and malic acids being present in smaller amounts. Carbohydrates occur chiefly in the form of sugars of which reducing sugars form the major part. Analysis of eight types of guava gave the following values (per 100 gms):

Citric acid	0.2-0.5 %
Reducing sugars	2.4-6.1%
Non-reducing sugars	0.5-5.7%
Tannins	0.1-0.4%
Pectin	0.3-1.6%

The tannin content is high in early stages of growth, and gradually decreases to a low value at the fully matured stage. Guava is poor in carotenoid pigments. The pulp of guava contains beta-carotene and Xanthophyll in equal proportions (total carotenoids-0.2 µg/g). The pink fleshed types are generally a better source of beta-carotene. Some pink fleshed guvava is also found to contain beta-carotene as well as very useful lycopene compound (an anti-oxidant).

Products/Preservation

Guava is used in the preparation of guava cheese, canned guava and guava jelly. Processes have also been developed for drying guavas as such and as pulp in the form of sheets, and also for the preparation of products such as guava juice and juice powder, guava concentrate, and guava nector.

Guava Cheese

Guava cheese is prepared from ripe and firm fruits. The fruits are washed and cut into small pieces, boiled in water and the pulp after straining to remove seeds and peels, is mixed with sugar and butter and heated until the material becomes thick. Citric acid, common salt and colouring matter are added. The whole product is allowed to set and then cut into pieces of attractive shapes. It is wrapped in butter paper and stored in a dry clean place.

Guava Jelly

For the preparation of guava jelly, healthy, rather tart fruits are taken. They are washed and cut into small pieces, and after the addition of citric acid, boiled in water for about half an hour. The juice is pressed out with a muslin cloth, and examined for the richness in pectin content. It is cooked with equal quantity of sugar till the resulting jelly boils at 105°. It is cooled thereafter.

Canned Guava

Fully ripe and firm fruits of white flesh and few seeds are chosen for canning. The fruits are peeled with a knife, cut into halves, and the seeds present are scooped out. The peeled cored fruits are kept immersed in 1-2% common salt solution to prevent browning, and canned in hot sugar syrup containing citric acid. Canned guavas often have a taste and aroma better than those of the fresh fruits. Loss of ascorbic acid (Vitamin C) during canning is about 19.4%. There is a gradual loss of ascorbic acid on storage. For 6, 12 & 24 months of storage, the loss of vitamin C would be 10.0, 18.3 & 39.5%, respectively.

Medicinal Uses

The guava plant as well as its fruits are considered medicinal.

(i) Extracts of fruit, flowers & leaves are found active against *Micrococcus pyogenes* and *Escherichia coli.*

(ii) Extracts of the fruit are found to be moderately active against enteric pathogens like *Salmonella typhosa* and *Shigella antidysenteriae.*

(iii) The fruit is tonic and is very nutritive, cooling and laxative.

(iv) The fruit is astringent in action and used against diarrhoea and dysentery.

(v) Full ripe fruit, if taken without crushing the seeds, removes obstinate constipation.

Jujube (Baer)

Botanical Name : *Zizyphus martiana*
Family Name : Rhamnaceae
Hindi Name : Baer
Sanskrit Name : Badarah
English Name : Jujube

Description

Jujube tree is small, evergreen but of variable size, up to 15 m or more with a spreading crown and stipular spines. Back rough, grey or dull block; leaves variable, oblong-elliptic, ovate or suborbicular, closely serrulate or entire, rounded at both ends, prominently 3-nerved; flowers greenish yellow, in axillary cynes; fruits oblong-globose or ovoid, red, orange or yellowish.

Distribution

Baer is found both wild and cultivated throughout the greater part of India, ascending to an altitude of 1,500 m in the Himalayas.

Parts Used

Fruit, leaves.

Properties

Astringent and stomachic.

Forms of Use

Fruit as such, leaves decoction.

Food Value

Baer fruit is eaten fresh. It is a good source of vitamin C and sugar and contains appreciable amount of mineral constituents. Analysis of the pulp of the fruit shows the following composition (per 100 gms):

Moisture	81.6%
Protein	0.8%

Fat	0.3%
Carbohydrates	17.0%
Minerals	0.3%
Calcium	4 mg
Phosphorus	9 mg
Iron	1.8 mg
β-carotene	0.021 I.U.
Thiamine (Vit. B_1)	0.02 mg
Riboflavin (Vit. B_2)	0.02 mg
Niacin	0.7 mg
Vitamin C	76 mg/100 g
Fluoride	0.1-0.2 p.p.m.
Pectin (as calcium pectate)	3.4%
Reducing sugar	1.4-6.2%
Non-reducing sugar	3.2-8.0%
Acidity (as citric acid)	0.2-1.1%

Citric acid is the major acid in the fruits, malic and oxalic acids being present in smaller amounts.

Products/Preservation

Large-sized fruits, which just begin to turn yellow, are chosen for canning. They are deeply pricked and soaked in 2 per cent common salt solution. The concentration of the salt solution is increased every day by about 2 per cent till it becomes 8 per cent. Fruits are then transferred to fresh 8 per cent salt solution, also containing 0.2 per cent of pot. meta-bi-sulphite, and stored for 1-3 months. The fruits are now washed in water till they become tender, and canned in the usual way in hot sugar syrup containing citric acid.

Medicinal Uses

(i) The unripe baer fruit increases thirst, lessens expectoration and biliousness.

(ii) The ripe fruit is sweet, sour, and has flavour, not good for digestion; causes diarrhoea in large doses.

(iii) The fruit is useful in fevers and for wounds and ulcers.

(iv) The seed is an aid to digestion.

(v) The dried ripe fruit is a mild laxative and expectorant.

(vi) The fruit seed is astringent; tonic to the heart and brain; allays thirst.

(vii) The berries are blood purifier and an aid to digestion.

(viii) An ointment made of the seeds with some bland oil is locally used as a liniment in rheumatism.

(ix) The plant is considered to have antitubercular properties.

(x) The seeds are also reported to have a sedative effect and recommended as a soporific.

(xi) They are also prescribed to stop nausea and vomiting and for relief from abdominal pain in pregnancy.

(xii) They are also given as an antidote to aconite poisoning, and used in poultices & other applications for wounds.

(xiii) The seeds are also used for the treatment of diarrhoea.

(xiv) Badri is mentioned in the list of oral contraceptives.

Lemon (Nebu)

Botanical Name : Citrus limon
Family Name : Rutaceae
Hindi Name : Nebu
Sanskrit Name : Nimbu
English Name : Lemon

Description

Lemon grows on a small thorny shrub/tree. Leaves ovate, petioles winged. Flowers tinged red. Fruit ovoid, yellow rind thin. It is an important health fruit of citrus group. Lemons and their juice have powerful antiseptic properties and are also good source of bioflavonoids and vitamin C.

Distribution

It is indigenous to western India. It reached Europe through Arabs. Now it is being cultivated all over the world.

Parts Used

Fruit.

Properties

Anti-scorbutic, appetiser, carminative, anti-flatulent, antacid, anti-diarrhoeal, anti-inflammatory, anti-pyorrhoea & dental caries etc.

Forms of Use

Leaves as paste, juice of fruit.

Food Value

It is rich in citric acid and also contains vitamin C. That's why it finds useful place in medicine. Its juice has a good keeping quality and can be preserved for a longer period.

Analysis (100 gms edible part) of lemon shows following composition:

Moisture	85%
Protein	1%
Fat	0.9%

Minerals	0.3%
Fibre	1.7%
Carbohydrates	11%
Calcium	70 mg
Phosphorus	10 mg
Iron	2.3 mg
Vitamin C	40 mg
Calorific Value	57

Also B-Complex, beta-carotene and oils etc.

Medicinal Uses

(i) A pale yellow volatile oil obtained from the fruit is bitter in taste, yet it is highly valued in medicine as a flavouring agent, carminative that relieves flatulence and treats gastric discomfort, and as stomachic, it improves appetite.

(ii) It is very useful against vitamin C deficiency, so it can be used against scurvy, a disease caused by lack of vitamin C.

(iii) It is highly beneficial for gums and teeths. It makes them strong and also prevents caries, inflammation and pyorrhoea.

(iv) It also corrects throat disorders such as catarrh, choking sensation and itch. A teaspoon juice of lemon plus two teaspoons honey should be licked after regular intervals.

(v) It is a very good medicine for eczema especially on the head part where hair is removed. Grind its skin on the affected part to get relief.

(vi) It also checks bleeding. Place a few drops of lemon juice on the bleeding part, bleeding will stop.

(vii) Take lemon juice daily in a glass of water to get rid of obesity and jaundice.

(viii) To correct upset stomach, take juice of one lemon in a glass of water and add a pinch of salt to it. Drink it to get relief soon.

(ix) A sufficient intake of lemon juice prevents the deposit of uric acid in the tissues and so reduces the possibility of an attack of gout.

(x) It is anti-influenza fruit. So, for bad cold, drink juice of lemon in a glass of luke warm water with one tea spoon honey. Repeat it two-three times.

(xi) Enlargement of spleen can be handled effectively with lemon juice. Two lemons juice morning and evening with a pinch of salt is sufficient for relief.

(xii) Its juice is also anti-cholesterol and make arteries clean, healthy and free from depositing cholesterol. It is regarded as a valuable food medicine in high blood pressure, arteriosclerosis, circulatory disorders and heart weakness.

(xiii) It is also useful in cholera as it has wonderful anticholera properties. Lemon juice can kill cholera bacilli within a very short time. It is also a very effective dependable food item against cholera during epidemic. Take lemon daily with food to keep cholera at bay.

(xiv) Foot and corn can be soothed with the help of lemon juice. Rubbing of the feet in warm water containing lemon juice provides soothing as well as refreshing feeling and opens pores of feet and induces sleep due to its relaxing action on the foot nerves.

(xv) As a beauty aid, lemon is regarded as a youth restorative and gives good look to our faces. Take juice of lemon, add sugar and borax in equal amount. Mix them to make a paste. Rub it on the face to remove pimples and black spots.

Lychee (Lichi)

Botanical Name : *Litchi chinensis*

Family Name : Annonaceae

Hindi Name : Lichi

English Name : Lychee

Description

Lychee grows on an evergreen tree, 10-12m high, with broad round-topped crown of glossy green foliage; leaves pinnate with 2-9 leaflets; flower polygamous, small, greenish-white or yellowish, in terminal panicles; fruit globose or oblong to ovate, 2.5 cm or more in diameter with a dark or light red or yellow rind, faintly or sharpy tubercled and brittle; fleshy-white, translucent, juicy, covering fully a large, dark brown, elliptic seed.

Distribution

Lychee is reported to have been introduced into India from China towards the end of the eighteenth century. It is now cultivated in a number of countries, outside China, including India, Burma, Indo-China, Thailand, Australia, New Zealand. India and South Africa are the largest producers other than China. Lychee is cultivated on acres of land in North Bihar, mostly in Muzaffarpur and Darbhanga district.

Parts Used

Fruit.

Forms of Use

Jam, jelly, fruit, juice.

Properties

Refreshing, nutritive, tonic & diuretic.

Food Value

The Lychee fruit consists of peel, aril and seed. The aril, which can be readily separated from seed, is soft and juicy with a delicious flavour and is generally eaten fresh. It yields

38.7-58.7% of juice containing total sugars (as invert sugar) 12.1-14.8%; reducing sugar 9.0-13.7%, non-reducing (sucrose, maltose) 1.0-3.4%; acidity (as citric acid) 0.72-0.36% and ascorbic acid 34.5-45.4 mg/100 g.

Analysis of fresh arils gave the following composition (per 100 gms):

Moisture	84.5%
Protein	1.0%
Fat	0.3%
Carbohydrate	13.6%
Fibre	0.4%
Mineral matter	0.5%
Calcium	10 mg
Phosphorus	30 mg
Nicotinic acid	0.4 mg
Ascorbic acid	247/100 g

Also contans vitamins B_1 and B_2

Products/Preservation

Lychee arils can be preserved by canning with syrup. In China, a solution of common salt is sprinkled over fruits to prevent rapid spoilage.

Lychee juice can be obtained by routine method, by adding preservatives like pot. meta-bi-sulphite in sugar syrup (66%).

Medicinal Uses

(i) Lychee seeds are used in China for intestinal trouble.

(ii) Lychee seeds are also used against anodyne and prescribed in neuralgic disorders and orchitis.

(iii) Fruit is said to be diuretic and digestive.

(iv) Fruits are very refreshing tonic.

Mango (Aam)

Botanical Name : *Magnifera indica*, Linn

Family Name : Anacardiaceae

Hindi Name : Aam

Sanskrit Name : Aamra

English Name : Mango

Description

Mango is the most popular and the choicest fruit of India and occupies a prominent place among the fruits of the world. Few other tropical fruits have the historic reputation like that of mango. Few others are so intimately connected with Indian folklore.

It grows on a large evergreen tree 10-14 m high with a heavy dome-shaped crown and a straight stout bole.

Distribution

Mango is by far the most important fruit crop of the country occupying about 50% of the total area (2 million acres) under fruits. It is cultivated in most parts of the Indian peninsula. It is common in subtropical Himalayas, hills of western and eastern ghats and forests of central India, Orissa, Assam and Andaman Islands.

Parts Used

Fruit, seeds, leaves and bark.

Properties

Ripe fruit laxative, diuretic, anti-haemorrhagic, refreshing, restorative, linthotropic, ophthalmic, astringent, anthelmintic, anti-diarrhoea, anti-syphilitic & tonic.

Forms of Use

Mango kernel, juice of ripe mango, unripe mango, unripe small mango (about torch bulb size), seed powder and boiled unripe mango etc.

Food Value

The mango fruit is one of the highly prized fruits of the tropics. It has rich aromatic flavour and is decent in taste having well blended mixture of acidity & sweetness. Unripe fruits are usually acidic and used for pickles, chutney, amchur and culinary preparations. Ripe fruits are preserved by canning or used in the manufacture of juice, squash, jams and jellies, preserves (murabba) and Ampapar (Amavat).

Analysis of the flesh of green & ripe mangoes gave the following composition (per 100 gms):

Contents	Green mango	Ripe mango
Moisture	90.0%	86.1%
Protein	0.7%	0.6%
Fat	0.1%	0.1%
Carbohydrate	8.8%	11.8%
Mineral matter	0.4%	0.3%
Calcium	0.01%	0.01%
Phosphorus	0.02%	0.02%
Iron	4.5 mg/100 g	3.0 mg/100 g
B-Carotene	1.50 I.U.	4,800 I.U.
Vitamin B_1	2 mg/100 g	8 mg/100 g
Vitamin B_2	30 ug	50 ug
Vitamin C	3 mg/100 g	13 mg/100 g
Niacin	2 mg/100 g	13 mg/100 g
Nicotinic acid	-	13 mg/100 g
Fibre	-	1.1%

The mango fruit also contains fluorine, iodine, copper, potassium, sulphur and magnesium.

The sugar and acid contents may vary as per condition and variety of mango. Sucrose, glucose, fructose are the principal carbohydrates present in ripe mango; maltose is also present. It has total sugars—11.20-16.80% with reducing sugars—1.40-4.83% with and non-reducing sugar—8.19-13.81%. Small amounts of cellulose, hemicelluloses and pectins are also present. The green tender fruit is rich in starch; during ripening the starch is hydrolysed into reducing sugars and a part of the latter is synthesised into sucrose. In the post-ripening stage, sucrose decomposes into reducing sugars.

Unripe fully developed mangoes of pickle variety contain citric, malic, oxalic, succinic acids besides two di & tri-basic acids; citric acid is the dominant constituent. As the fruit ripens, acid content decreases to more than half.

Among amino acids, mango has asparatic acid, glutamic acid, alanine, glycine, methionine, leucine and cystein.

Products/Preservation

(a) ***Dried Slices*** – Immature mangoes are cut into pieces, mixed with salt (6-8%) and dried in the sun. The dried product is packed in wooden *peti* or box and used in the preparation of chutney & pickles.

A popular method of preserving unripe mango is to cut the peeled material into thin slices and leave it to dry in the sun; slices may be seasoned with turmeric powder before drying. Known as Amchur, the dried material is used as such or after grinding into powder. The powder keeps well for about 3 years if packed in air-tight containers. Amchur is used as a souring agent for soup, chutney & vegetables.

(b) ***Mango Chutney*** – Unripe mango is used for this preparation. Peeled slices are softened by heating with a small amount of water. Sugar, salt, red chilli powder, ginger & other spices (cardamom, cinnamon, cumin etc.) are added and the mixture cooked over slow fire till it becomes fairly thick. Vinegar is then added and cooking continued till the desired consistency is obtained. In some preparations, dry fruits are also added.

(c) ***Mango Pickle (Achaar)*** – To make mango pickle, slices of unripe mango, mustard oil, fenugreek, turmeric, fennel, powdered red chilli, salt and pepper are needed. All the ingredients are mixed together and stored for quite some time in mustard oil till pulp softens.

(d) ***Canned Mango*** – Firm ripe mango fruits are selected for canning. After washing, the fruit is peeled and the flesh cut into long pieces of almost equal size. The pieces or slices are placed in brine (2%) to prevent browning & canned in hot sugar syrup containing 0.3%-0.5% citric acid. Mango pulp obtained by squeezing out the juice from ripe fruits is canned in the same way as slices. Trimmings are used in the preparation of jams & squashes. Canned mangoes are a good source of B-Carotene (Vitamin A) and ascorbic acid (Vitamin C). The vitamins are well retained in canned pieces.

(e) ***Mango Leather (Aam Papar, Amawat)*** – Mango pulp dried in the form of sheets or slabs is commonly called mango leather or mango bread (Aam Papar). The juice from full ripe or slightly over-ripe mangoes is squeezed out, strained through cloth and spread in thin layers over mat smeared with mustard oil and dried in the sun. The product is exposed to sulphur fumes before packing.

(f) ***Juice Powder*** – It is prepared by concentrating the mango juice, blending with sugars, fruit acids etc. and drying in a vacuum shelf drier. The dried material is powdered and packed in air-tight containers with or without inpackage desiccants. The product is a rich source of vitamins and can be used in the preparation of ice-creams and food for infants and invalids. It can be reconstituted into juice and used as a beverage.

(g) ***Mango Custard Powder*** – It is obtained from mango pulp mixed with skimmed milk powder, sugar, corn starch & other ingredients. The blend is dried to 1-1.5% moisture & ground to a granular powder. It contains Moisture 1.3%, Protein 7-1%, Fat 0.17%, Starch 3.6%, Sugar 18.4%, Fibre 1.5%, Ash 2.6%, Iron 6.6 mg, P 204.0 mg, Ca 238 mg, Vitamin C 32.8 mg, β-carotene (Vitamin A) 12,000 μg/100g; acidity 1.18%.

Medicinal Uses

(i) Ripe mango fruit is considered invigorating, refreshing and fattening. The juice along with aromatics is recommended as a restorative tonic.

(ii) It is a powerful nutritive fruit, containing most of essential substances needed by our body.

(iii) It contains vitamins and minerals along with important chemicals that can keep our body fit and fine. So, it is a complete natural food.

(iv) Unripe mango (of about torch bulb size) if used 6 pieces at a time per day for a week, clears all stones from kidney. This should be repeated consecutively 3 years in mango season.

(v) A drink made from boiled unripe mango with salt and sugar is a wonderful remedy for heat stroke.

(vi) Powdered mango seed when taken 3 times a day cures diarrhoea and dysentery.

(vii) Mango juice and milk is a restorative tonic. It should be taken throughout the season to stay healthy.

(viii) Toothpowder prepared from mango leaves keeps teeth healthy.

(ix) The gum obtained from mango tree is used for dressing cracked feet and for scabies. It is also considered anti-syphilitic.

(x) Sun-dried slices of the unripe fruit are excellent remedy for scurvy.

(xi) The resinous liquid, oozing out at the cut end of the stalk of a fruit about to ripen, mixed with lime juice is a useful dressing for scabies and other skin diseases.

(xii) The skin of the unripe fruit is given with sugar in menses disturbance; the skin is astringent and a stimulant tonic; its powder is given with milk and honey for bleeding dysentery and as a tonic for the digestive organs.

(xiii) The ripe fruit is laxative, diuretic and useful in haemorrhage of uterus, lungs & intestines.

(xiv) The sind of the fruit is astringent, stimulant and used as a tonic in debility.

(xv) Its juice, if snuffed, is said to stop nasal bleeding.

Watermelons (Tarbuz and Kharbuza)

Botanical Name : *Citrullus vulgaris & cucumis melo*
Family Name : Cucurbitaceae
Hindi Name : Tarbuz Kharbuza
English Name : Water-melon & Milk-melon

Description

Both the fruits are widely cultivated in India and other countries also. They are available in summers and impart a wonderful hydrating effect to our body. Their juices are very nutritive and refreshing. Analysis shows the following composition of two types of melons:

Melon-Water (100 gm)		**Melon-Milk (100 gm)**	
Moisture	96%	Moisture	90%
Protein	0.2 %	Protein	0.3%
Fat	0.2%	Fat	0.2%
Fibre	0.2%	Fibre	0.4%
Carbohydrates	3.5%	Carbohydrates	3.5%
Calcium	11 mg	Calcium	32 mg
Phosphorus	12 mg	Phosphorus	14 mg
Iron	7.4 mg	Iron	1.4 mg
Vitamin C	26 mg	Vitamin C	30 mg
and Vitamin B-Complex Carotene and anthocyanins		and Vitamin B-Complex & β-Carotene etc.	
Calorific Value	16	Calorific value	17

Medicinal Uses

(i) They are wonderful diuretic agents. They are of great value in diseases like jaundice, typhoid and nephritis.

Orange (Santara)

Botanical Name : *Citrus aurantium*
Family Name : Rutaceae
Hindi Name : Santara
Sanskrit Name : Narangah
English Name : Orange

Description

Orange is a beautiful gift of nature. It is one of the popular fruits of citrus family. It is very delicious and nourishing fruit.

Distribution

Orange is a native of China, introduced in India by Vasco-da-Gama in 1498 but the present varieties were introduced from other countries. Extensively cultivated all over the world, orange grows in India widely in Nagpur, Pune & Assam.

Parts Used

Fruit.

Properties

Anti-scorbutic, nutritive, cardio-tonic, anti-pyorrhoea and dental caries, carminative etc.

Forms of Use

Juice.

Food Value

Starch of the orange is predigested food which changes into readily assimilable sugar by sun rays. That's why it is readily absorbed in the blood. It produces heat and energy in the body immediately after its use.

Daily use of orange juice prevents common cold, influenza and bleeding gums. It keeps one healthy and strong and contributes towards longevity. Orange juice suits young & old and can be recommended in all kinds of diseases.

Analysis of 100 gms edible part of orange gives the following composition:

Moisture	87.6%
Protein	0.7%
Fat	0.2%
Minerals	0.3%
Fibre	0.3%
Carbohydrates	11%
Calcium	26 mg
Phosphorus	20 mg
Iron	0.3 mg
Vitamin C	30 mg
Calorific Value	60

Some vitamins of B-Complex

Medicinal Uses

(i) ***Fever*** – Orange is an excellent food in all types of fever when the digestive power of the body is seriously disturbed. Orange juice is the most ideal liquid food in fevers like typhoid, TB and measles. It gives energy, increases urinary output and promotes body resistance against infections, thereby helping to recover fast.

(ii) ***Dyspepsia*** – Orange is a good food remedy in chronic dyspepsia. It gives rest to the digestive organ and supplies nutrition in the most easily assimilable form. It also stimulates the flow of digestive juices thereby improving digestion and increasing appetite. It creates favourable conditions for the development of friendly bacteria in the intestines.

(iii) ***Constipation*** – Taking one or two oranges at bed time and again on getting up in the morning, is an excellent way of stimulating the bowel action thus removing food residue from the colon which may cause putrefaction and intoxication.

(iv) ***Bone and Teeth*** – Being a good source of calcium and vitamin C, orange works well in the diseases of the bone and teeth. Many patients of pyorrhoea and dental caries have been cured by taking large amounts of orange juice.

(v) ***Children's Ailments*** – Orange juice is considered to be the best food for infants if 15 to 120 ml of it is given daily to them. It prevents scurvy and rickets and helps growth. It is good for babies whose normal development is retarted for some cause.

(vi) ***Heart Disease*** – Orange juice sweetened with honey, is highly useful in heart diseases. In cardiac conditions like coronary ischaemia and infarction, its juice is recommended.

(vii) ***As Expectorant*** – The use of orange mixed with a pinch of salt and a tablespoon of honey is effective remedy for TB, asthma, common cold, bronchitis and another condition of cough associated with difficult expectorations. It eases expectorations and protects from secondary infections.

(viii) ***Acne*** – The orange peel is valuable in the treatment of pimples and acne. The peel, pounded well with water on a piece of stone, should be applied on the acne-affected area.

Note – Mosambi *(Citrus sinensis)* is another useful fruit that belongs to the family of orange. It purifies the blood and corrects digestion and works as a tonic for heart. Its juice is highly beneficial for the patients suffering from chronic diseases for a long time. It provides strength to the body and protects it from further deterioration.

Analysis of 100 gms of edible part of Mosambi gives the following composition: (Moisture-84.6%, Protein 1.5%, Fat 1%, Carbohydrates 11%, Iron 1.5%, Calcium 0.09%, Phosphorus 0.02%, Vitamin A-26, Vitamin C-63).

Papaya (Papita)

Botanical Name : *Carica papaya*

Family Name : Caricaceae

Hindi Name : Papita

Sanskrit Name : Brahmai-randah

English Name : Papaya

Description

Papaya is one of the most valuable tropical fruits. It is large and fleshy. Its weight varies from 1/2 to 2 kg and is pear-shaped. Its central cavity may contain seeds or may be seedless. On ripening, it becomes yellow and sweet in taste.

Distribution

Papaya has its origin in Mexico and Costa Rica. It is now widely cultivated in India and mostly in all countries of the world. It has a typical aroma and delicious taste.

Parts Used

Fruit.

Properties

Cardio-tonic, carminative, digestant, anti-constipation, anthelmintic, anti-haemorrhoidal etc.

Forms of Use

Fruit is eaten.

Food Value

Papaya is a wholesome fruit containing proteins, minerals, vitamins, carotenes etc. Its carbohydrate content is mainly of invert sugar which is a form of predigested food.

Analysis of 100 gms edible part of papaya gives the following composition (per 100 gm of edible portion):

Moisture	91%
Protein	0.6%
Fat	0.1%
Minerals	0.5%
Fibre	0.8%
Carbohydrates	7.2%
Calcium	17 mg
Phosphorus	13 mg
Vitamin C	57 mg
Iron	0.5 mg
Calorific Value	32

Small amount of Vitamin B-Complex

Medicinal Uses

(i) It has established medicinal values from the ancient times. It is not only one of the most easily digested fruits but also aids in digestion of other foods.

(ii) Ripe papaya is an excellent tonic for growing children, pregnant women and nursing mothers. It is an energy-giving food.

(iii) Papaya contains protein-digesting enzyme in the milky juice or latex, which flows in a network of nerves in the whole plant. This enzyme is like that of pepsin and its digestive action is so powerful that it can digest 200 times its own weight in protein. Its effect is to assist the body's own enzymes in assimilating the maximum nutritional value from food to provide energy and body building material.

(iv) ***Intestinal Disorders*** – Papain in the raw papaya is highly beneficial in the deficiency of gastric juice, excess of unhealthy mucus in the stomach, in dyspepsia and intestinal irritation. The ripe fruit, if eaten regularly, corrects habitual constipation, bleeding piles and chronic diarrhoea. The juice of the papaya seeds is also useful in dyspepsia and bleeding piles.

(v) ***Round Worms*** – The digestive enzyme papain in the milky juice of the unripe papaya is a powerful anthelmentic (it destroys roundworms). A tablespoonful of the fresh juice and equal quantity of honey should be mixed with 3/4 tsf of hot water and taken as a dose by an adult followed by 30 ml castor oil in 250 ml milk. Repeat it two times.

(vi) ***In Menses*** – The unripe papaya helps the contraction of the muscle fibres of the womb and is thus useful in regulating improper menstrual flow.

(vii) ***Liver and Spleen*** – It is liver corrective and useful in cirrhosis of the liver caused by alcohol and malnutrition. Ripe papaya is highly valuable in enlargement of the spleen. The fruit should be peeled off, cut into pieces and dipped in vinegar for a week and after that, 2/3 pieces should be taken with meals. In Malaria also, spleen sometimes increases.

Peach (Aru)

Botanical Name : *Prunus persica*

Family Name : Rosaceae

Hindi Name : Aru

English Name : Peach

Description

Peach grows on a small tree up to 8m high with glabrous twigs, leaves oblong to broad lanceolate, serrate, glabrous, flowers solitary, pink; fruits subglobose, 5-7 cm across, fleshy, with a hard and deeply pitted stone.

Distribution

Peach is believed to be a native of China. In India, peaches are grown in Kashmir, Himachal Pradesh, Kullu, Kumaun hills and Punjab.

Parts Used

Fruit, leaves.

Properties

Stomachic, demulcent, anti-scorbutic, anthelmintic.

Forms of Use

Fruit is eaten raw.

Food Value

Peaches are a fair source of sugars, thiamine (Vitamin B_1) and ascorbic acid (Vitamin C) and retinol (Vitamin A). Ripe peaches contain 88 per cent of edible matter as shown by the following composition obtained by the analysis of peaches (per 100 gms):

Moisture	86%
Protein	1.2%
Fat	0.3%

Fibre	1.2%
Carbohydrate	10.5%
Minerals	0.8%
Calcium	15.0 mg
Magnesium	21.0 mg
Iron	2.4 mg
Phosphorus	41 mg
Sodium	2 mg
Potassium	453 mg
Copper	0.06 mg
Sulphur	26 mg
Vitamin A	450 I.U.
Thiamine	0.02 mg
Riboflavin	0.03 mg
Nicotonic acid	0.5 mg
Ascorbic acid	6.0 mg

The acids present in peach are mainly malic and citric acids.

Products/Preservation

Peaches are a favourite table fruit. They are soft and juicy when ripe and are mostly used as desserts. They become very delicious when cooked in syrup, and are mostly used for canning. Various preparations are canned peach, peach nector, dried peach.

Medicinal Uses

(i) Fruits are given in stomach ailments.

(ii) Its juice is known to remove worms from the intestine.

(iii) It is very useful in keeping eyes healthy.

Pear (Naspati)

Botanical Name : *Pyrus communis*
Family Name : Rosaceae
Hindi Name : Naspati
English Name : Pear

Description

Pear grows on a tree with a broad pyramidal crown, leaves orbicular-ovate to elliptic, crenate-serrate, flowers white, in few flowered corymbs, fruits variable, turbinate or subglobose, calyx lobes persistent, the flesh with gritty concretions.

Distribution

Pear is grown in the temperate regions of Europe and West Asia. In India, it is cultivated on small scale (as compared to apple) in Punjab, Kashmir, Himachal Pradesh, Chennai, Assam, Bengal and U.P.

Parts Used

Fruit.

Properties

Astringent, sedative, febrifuge.

Forms of Use

Fruit eaten raw.

Food Value

Pears are consumed in India primarily as fresh fruit. A sample of pear contains: acid (as malic acid), 0.24%; reducing sugar, 8.2%; total sugars (as invert sugar), 10.8%. The minerals in pears include—boron, copper, molybdenum, zinc, cobalt, arsenic, fluorine and iodine.

Reducing sugars, of which fructose is the major component, constitute over 80% of the total sugar present in pears.

Analysis of the edible portion of pear gives the following composition (per 100 gms):

Moisture	86.3%
Protein	0.2
Fat	0.2
Minerals	0.2
Fibre	1.4
Carbohydrate	11.7/100 g
Calcium	10 mg
Phosphorus	10 mg
Iron	1.5 mg
Vitamin	9 I.U.
Thiamine (Vit. B_1)	0.03 mg
Riboflavin (Vit. B_2)	0.02 mg
Nicotinic acid	0.02 mg
Vitamin C	7 mg

Pear also contains a number of important amino acids apart from biotin (Vitamin H), pantho-thenic acid, folic acid and vitamin B_{12}.

Products/Preservation

Canned pear, pear juice and dried pear are the products prepared from firm ripe pears.

For canned pear, fruits are peeled and cut into halves, and core removed. They are then kept in salt solution (1-2%) to prevent browning, syruped, sterlized and then promptly cooled in cans. Syrup-packed canned pears contain: Water, 81.1%; protein, 1.2%; fat, 0.1%; carbohydrate, 18.4%; fibre, 0.8% and ash, 0.2%.

Juice obtained from ripe pears has excellent flavour. It is used in jellies and sherbets and after acidification as beverage and bear nectar.

Dried pear is prepared by sun-drying of pears, cut, sulphured and again kept in the sun for a day or two. Dried pear contains: Protein, 4.4-5.1%; Carbohydrate, 63.2-64.2%; and ash 1.2-1.4%; calcium, 25-29mg; phosphorus, 29.2-39.2 mg; iron, 0.25-0.64% and potassium, 543-741 mg, 543-741 mg; beta-carotene (as vitamin A), 20 IU/100 g.

Medicinal Uses

(i) Pears are a good source of pectin, containing fair amount of invert sugars and thiamine (Vitamin B_1).

(ii) They are reported to help in maintaining a desirable acid-base balance in the human body.

(iii) Pears have been recommended to patients suffering from diabetes because of their low sucrose content.

(iv) They are also found to be fever reducing.

(v) They are slightly sedative in action, and induce sleep when taken too much.

Pineapple (Anannas)

Botanical Name : *Ananas Comosus, L.*

Family Name : Bromeliaceae

Hindi Name : Anannas

Sanskrit Name : Anannas

English Name : Pineapple

Description

This is a small genus of five species, native to tropical America. A. comosus, the polymorphic species, is cultivated widely in tropical countries for its succulent fruit.

The pineapple plant is a perennial, erect herb, with a short stem bearing a rosette of leaves 2-3 ft. long, with prickly margins and spiny tips. The fruit, which has a rough surface and a crown of small leaves, has succulent flesh of yellow to light orange colour.

Distribution

Pineapple is indigenous to Brazil. It was introduced into India about the middle of the 16th century. It is cultivated in Assam, Bengal and along the West coast. Hawaii and Malaya are the largest pineapple producing countries.

The fruit matures quickly and possesses good taste and flavour. Its average weight is 1.5-2 kg.

Although pineapple can be grown under a variety of conditions, it thrives best in places having a mild and humid tropical climate. It flourishes best in places where the annual rainfall is about 50 inches, evenly distributed throughout the year.

Parts Used

Ripe, unripe fruits and leaves.

Properties

Astringent, digestive, abortifacient, anthemintic, purgative, cooling, diuretic & febrifuge.

Forms of Use

Fruit juice.

Food Value

Findings of pineapple analysis are as follows:

Edible fruit portion	65.7%
Refuse	33.4%
Juice	19.2%

It is found that pineapple juice contains 4.3% of total sugar. However, the sugar content of juice varies from 8-15% and the acid content from 0.3-0.9%. Further analysis gives the following composition (per 100 gms):

Moisture	86.5%
Protein	0.6%
Fat	0.3%
Fibre	0.5%
Carbohydrates	12.0%
Mineral matter	0.5%
Calcium	00.2 mg
Phosphorus	0.02 mg
Niacin	0.1 mg
Iron	10 mg
Vitamin A	60 I.U.
Vitamin C	63 mg
Calories/K cal	46

Products/Preservation

After harvesting, the fruit is carefully graded according to size and maturity and packed in boxes or crates for transport. Mature green fruits keep well for about a month at room temperature. A large part of the crop is canned. The pineapple juice from the trimmings, after treatment with lime, is used for the canning syrup. In some cases, however, the appearance of the canned fruit suffers slightly on account of removal of the deep set eyes and the fibrous nature of the flesh. The trimmings can be converted into pineapple jam, or pineapple syrup of good taste and flavour. The syrup can be blended with other fruit juices to produce fruit beverages.

Medicinal Uses

(i) Fresh pineapple juice contains bronelin, an enzyme which aids digestion. This is destroyed on heating to 65° and above.

(ii) Pineapple juice is found to be very refreshing and cooling. It tones up body systems.

(iii) It is also anthelmintic in nature.

(iv) Pineapple juice from unripe fruits acts as violent purgative.

(v) It is also an abortifacient.

(vi) To get rid of indigestion, sprinkle black pepper & salt over small pieces of anannas and take 3-4 times in a day.

(vii) To get rid of swelling over the body, take one full ripe anannas daily for 15 days.

(viii) To get rid of stones, use anannas juice daily for 15 days and, if required, one month.

(ix) Fresh juice is diuretic, diaphoretic, aperient and helps in the digestion of albuminous substances.

(x) Juice of the unripe anannas is acrid, styptic, powerful dimetic emmenagogue.

(xi) Fruit juice is given to ally—soothing gastric irritability in fever & in jaundice.

(xii) Juice of unripe anannas shows promising antifertility property.

Plum (Alubukhara)

Botanical Name : *Prunus domestica*
Family Name : Rosaceae
Hindi Name : Alubukhara
Sanskrit Name : Arukam
English Name : Plum

Description

Plum grows on a small tree, with twigs pubescent when young; flowers white, usually in clusters; fruits firm in texture, varying in colour from green and golden yellow to red and dark purple; stones large, rough or pitted.

Of all the stone fruits, plums are the most varied and include a large range of types varying in plant habit, leaf size and form, flowering habit and fruit characteristic quality.

Distribution

Plum originates in Europe, Japan and North America. In India, it is cultivated in Himachal Pradesh and Chaubattia in U.P.

Parts Used

Fruit.

Properties

Laxative, refrigerant, antileucorrhoeic, tonic.

Forms of Use

Fruit is eaten as such.

Food Value

Plum contains appreciable amounts of sugars and beta-carotene (Vitamin A). Analysis of the edible portion (90-93%) of the fruit of the red plums gave the following composition (per 100 gms):

Moisture	86.3%
Protein	0.7%

Fat	0.4%
Fibre	0.4%
Carbohydrate	11.7%
Minerals	0.5%
Calcium	10 mg
Phosphorus	20 mg
Iron	1.4 mg
Potassium	190 mg
Copper	0.05 mg
Nicotinic acid	0.1 mg
Ascorbic acid	5 mg
Vitamin A	983 I.U.

The ripening of the plum is characterised by softening of the flesh, development of pigment, marked increase in sugars and relatively smaller decrease in acid content. The acid content is due to citric acid, although small amount of tartaric & malic acids have been found. Sugars present are glucose (3.0-6.2%), fructose (2.7-6.1%) and sucrose (0.7-4.8%). The aroma of plum blossoms mainly due to benzaldehyde.

Products/Preservation

Plums are used as desserts; they are cooked and eaten, canned and dried, and also made into jams. Certain types of plums are dried & called as Prunes.

Medicinal Uses

(i) It is demulcent, mildly laxative and refrigerant. It is often added to decoctions to improve their flavour and promote their effect.

(ii) Its juice is very cooling and is given in fever etc.

Pomegranate (Anar)

Botanical Name : *Punica granatum, L*

Family Name : Puniaceae

Hindi Name : Anar

Sanskrit Name : Dadimah

English Name : Pomegranate

Description

Pomegranate is a fruit of great antiquity and is known to have been cultivated in the Middle East more than 5000 years ago. The wild or semi-wild pomegranate still exists in the north of Syria, Iran, Afghanistan and Baluchistan.

A shrub or small tree 5-10m high, bark smooth, dark grey; leaves 2.0-8.0 cm long, oblong or obovate, shining above; flowers usually deep red, sometimes yellow, 3.7-5.0 cm long, mostly solitary or 2-4 together; fruits globose, crowned by persistent calyx, with a coriaceous woody sind and an interior separated with membranous walls, containing numerous seeds; seeds angular with a fleshy festa which is red, pink and whitish.

Distribution

Cultivated throughout India.

Parts Used

Ring of the fruit.

Properties

Tonic, anthelmintic, antidysenteric, cooling.

Forms of Use

Decoction, fruit juice etc.

Food Value

Pomegranate is largely used as a dessert. The seeds along with the fleshy portions are dried and commercially marketed as anardana which is widely used as a condiment.

Analysis of the edible portion (68%) of pomegranate gave the following composition (per 100 gms of the edible part):

Moisture	78.0%
Protein	1.6%
Fat	0.1%
Fibre	5.1%
Carbohydrate	14.5%
Mineral matter	0.7%
Calcium	10 mg
Magnesium	12 mg
Oxalic Acid	14 mg
Phosphorus	70 mg
Iron	0.3 mg
Sodium	0.9 mg
Potassium	13.30 mg
Copper	0.2 mg
Sulphur	12.0 mg
Chlorine	2.0 mg
Thiamine (B_1)	0.06 mg
Riboflavin	0.10 mg
Nicotinic acid	0.30 mg
Vitamin C	14 mg

Pomegranate is a good source of sugars and vitamin C, and fair source of iron but poor in calcium. The sugar content increases with the age of the fruit and of the tree. The fruit contains 0.27% of pectin (as calcium pectate). During ripening the insoluble pectin changes into soluble pectin. The concentration of Vitamin C is said to increase with maturity and ripening of the fruit.

Glucose and fructose (reducing sugars) are the principal sugars in pomegranate juice. Sucrose is absent but maltose is reported. The acids consist primarily of citric acid with malic as the minor component. Among the amino acids, asparatic acid and glutamic have been identified in the juice.

Products/Preservation

A delicious juice is prepared from pomegranate. Fully ripe fruits yield a sweet, deep coloured juice with a rich flavour. For obtaining juice, the grains are separated from the fruit and processed in a basket press. The juice after filtration is clarified by heating in a flash pasteurizer to 79-82% and then cooled immediately. It is preserved by addition of sodium benzoate. The preserved juice has an excellent keeping quality.

The quality of pomegranate juice is determined to a great extent by its acids and sugar contents. The acidity of the juice varies from 7.8 to 3.47 g/100 ml and reducing sugars from 7.8 to 13.7 g/100 ml. Fruits of the *Kandhari* type produce a purplish red juice with a mildly acid-sweet taste. It looks very attractive and is a powerful refreshing drink.

Pomegranate juice blends well with other juices. It may be converted into an excellent syrup. *Anar Rub* is a product locally prepared from the juice by adding sugar and heating to a thick, viscous consistency. It keeps well and is used like tomato sauce or ketchup.

The fruit juice easily ferments and may be used for the production of wines. The juice of the wild pomegranates in Russia is used in the manufacture of citric and sodium citrate for medicinal use.

Medicinal Uses

(i) Fresh pomegranate juice is used as an ingredient of cooling and refrigerant mixtures and of some medicines for dyspepsia.

(ii) The juice of the leaves and the young fruit, and the decoction of the bark are used in dysentery.

(iii) The sweet types of pomegranate are said to be mildly laxative, while the less sweet types are believed to be good in inflammation of stomach and in heart pain.

(iv) Sherbet of the ripe fruit is given in typhus, gastric and asthmatic fever, inflammation of the urinary tract and haemorrhage.

(v) Grains of fruit with black pepper & salt are given in jaundice.

(vi) Pomegranate juice with lime juice taken 2/3 times daily corrects liver dysfunction and jaundice.

(vii) *Anardana,* a preparation from pomegranate is used against dyspepsia and stomach-ache.

Strawberry (Rasbhari)

Botanical Name : *Fragaria chiloensis*
Family Name : Rosaceae
Hindi Name : Rasbhari
English Name : Strawberry

Description

A stout stoloniferous herb with long arching runners, leaves thick, blunt toothed, bluish green more or less glossy above and pale below, flowers white, borne in small clusters; fruit varying in shape, fairly large, scarlet, covered with achenes which do not project much outside the surface.

Distribution

A small genus of low perennial creeping herbs, strawberry is distributed in the wild state in the temperate and sub-tropical regions of the world. Four species are recorded in India, viz. F. daltoniana, F. nilgerrensis, F. vesca and F. chiloensis.

The majority of the cultivated forms have been derivatives of F. chiloensis, a native of the Pacific coast of North and South America.

Strawberry is essentially a crop of the higher elevations in India and its cultivation is confined to certain parts of Kashmir, Punjab, U.P., Mumbai, Chennai and Mysore.

Parts Used

Fruit.

Properties

Refreshing, nutritive, tonic, astringent, diuretic.

Forms of Use

Fruit, juice.

Food Value

Ripe strawberries are bright red in colour with a soft melting flesh of sweetish flavour. They are esteemed as dessert and consumed not so much for their food value, as for their flavour. Strawberries are ranked high among "small fruits."

Analysis of fresh Indian strawberry gave the following composition (100 gms):

Moisture	87.8%
Protein	0.7%
Mineral matter	0.4%
Fat	0.2%
Fibre	1.1%
Carbohydrate	9.8%
Calcium	0.3 mg
Phosphorus	0.03 mg
Iron	1.8 mg
Vitamin C	52 mg
Nicotinic acid	0.2 mg

Strawberry is richer in vitamin C (50-90 mg/100 g) than orange and lemon. The vitamin C content is particularly high in fresh fruits of rich flavour. Other vitamins reported to be present are: thiamine (Vitamin B_1) (0.5 mg/100 g) and riboflavin (Vitamin B_2) (0.08 mg/100 g). Sugars (mostly reducing sugars, i.e. glucose & fructose) make up 70-80% of the total soluble solids and 50% of the total solids.

Strawberries contain pectin (as calcium pectate), 0.l54% and organic acids (citric and malic), 0.7-1.6%.

The mineral constituents of the fruits are: Copper (0.02 mg/ 100 g of fruit) and iodine (0.01-0.03 mg/100 g of fresh fruit). The flavour of the fruit is attributed to the presence of volatile esters. Salicylic acid has been frequently identified in distilled juices, most often as methyl salicylate (as claimed). The pigment responsible for the deep red colour is anthocyanins.

Products/Preservation

Strawberry juice contains: total solids, 7.71%; acids (as citric), 0.71%; invert sugar, 4.46%; sucrose, 0.24%; tannin, 0.13%; and ash 0.43%.

Large quantities of strawberry are quickly frozen, sliced or whole with sugar. Strawberries may be made into preserves, jams, jellies or syrup; they may also be canned. Fresh strawberries and strawberry syrup are used in soda-fountain beverages and ice creams. Strawberry wine is prepared by adding sugar to crushed fruit or juice, fermenting the mass with or without the addition of yeast, straining the liquid and storing for use as wine.

Medicinal Uses

(i) The leaves are mildly astringent and diuretic.

(ii) As strawberry contains vitamin C more than lemon and orange, it can be used against scurvy.

(iii) It is a refreshing tonic.

Fruit Juices and Their Preservation

In India, cold drinks are in demand practically all the year round. Among these, fruit juices have an important place. Being rich in essential minerals, vitamins and other nutritive factors, they are quite popular. The nutritive value of fruit juices is far greater than that of synthetic products which are at present being bottled and sold in large quantities throughout the year. If real fruit juices could be substituted for these synthetic preparations, it would be a boon to the consumer as well as to the fruit grower. There is, therefore, great scope in the country for the production of fruit juices and allied products.

With the rapid progress in fruit farming during the last two decades, fresh juices are increasingly sold by vendors in large cities and towns. The demand for fresh juices is on the increase, but these cannot be had easily during off-season of their fruits. Therefore, fruit juices have to be preserved in a form in which they can be made available to the public during off-season.

Till about 20 years ago, only grapes and apple juices were produced, and these juices were used almost exclusively for medicinal purposes. These were generally recommended by doctors for infants and invalids. Now-a-days, however, due to common use of fruit-juices as breakfast foods etc., a large variety of them is produced on a big scale from fruits such as orange, pineapple, grape, apple, pomegranate, lemon, mango, mosambi, banana, peach and plum etc. They are now becoming more popular than the carbonated beverages from apples and grapes.

In our country, the pure fruit juice industry is still in its infancy. Preparation of these juices is limited to small scale. Production of best quality fruit juice requires costly equipment. Recently, few units have taken up fruit juice production on a large scale without compromising with their nutritional properties.

Fruit juices, especially orange, apple and grape juices, are concentrated using modern equipment so that there should not be any loss in their nutritional value and flavour. Sometimes, the required flavour is added back to the concentrates to get full fruit taste and flavour on dilution for serving. These concentrates are used as basis for soft drinks, medicinal preparations, baby foods, tonic foods etc. The frozen orange juice concentrate (four to one) is an excellent example in this case. Concentration is effected by freezing or by application of heat employing high vacuum etc. Fruit juice and concentrates are further converted into free-flowing fruit juice powders by puff drying. Sometimes, sealed in flavours are blended with the powders so as to get natural fruit juices on reconstitution for serving as beverages etc.

Preservation of Fruit Juices

Freshly extracted juices are highly attractive in appearance and possess good taste and aroma, but deteriorate rapidly, if kept for some time. This is due to:

(a) Fermentation (by mould yeast & bacteria).

(b) Enzymes present in juice affect colour and flavour (e.g. apple juice turns brown after some time due to oxidative enzyme).

(c) Chemicals present in juice may inter-react to spoil taste and aroma.

(d) Juices on exposure to air, turn bitter due to some reaction.

(e) Metal used for extraction or storing may spoil taste and flavour.

To retain the natural taste and aroma of the juice, it is necessary to preserve it soon after extraction by these methods:

1. Pasteurisation
2. Addition of chemicals
3. Addition of sugar

4. Freezing & drying
5. Carbonation etc.

Pasteurisation

Preservation of fruit juices by heat is the most popular method. Here juice is heated at high temperature, say 80-100°, for a short time to kill bacteria followed by cooling and packing in boiled containers and sealing.

Preservation with Chemicals

Preservation with the help of chemicals keeps the juice free from spoilage for a longer period of time. These chemicals are sodium benzoate, potassium meta-bisulphite (used as a source of sulphur dioxide), citric acid, acetic acid and ascorbic acid etc. But their uses should be within the limit (for 1000 g juice, 4-5 g chemical is used).

Preservation with Sugar

Fruit juices containing 66 per cent or more of sugar do not ordinarily ferment. Sugar absorbs most of the available water; consequently, water is not available for the growth of bacteria. It is very difficult to induce fermentation in highly concentrated sugar solutions. Sugar syrups containing 66 per cent sugar (sp. gr. 1.330) have so little moisture available for micro-organisms to grow. Thus sugar acts as a preservative by osmosis and not as a true poison for bacteria. Citric acid is also added to sugar solution because it prevents crystallisation of sugar and converts it into invert sugar (glucose + fructose).

Preservation by Freezing

The best way of preserving pure fruit juices is by freezing. The properly frozen juice retains its freshness, colour and aroma for a long time. This method is especially useful in the case of juices whose flavour is adversely affected by heating.

Preservation by Drying

It is done in the same way as milk drying.

Preservation by Carbonation & Filtration

Moulds and yeasts require oxygen for their growth. As they

are aerobic, they become inactive in the presence of carbon dioxide. Although carbonated beverages contain sugar much below 66 per cent, the absence of air and presence of carbon dioxide in them help to prevent the growth of mould and yeast.

Pure fruit juices like orange juice, apple juice, pineapple juice etc. which are highly prized as nutritive foods, are packed in large quantities in many countries. Apple juice is generally bottled, while other juices are canned.

Apple Juice

In our country, demand for apple juice is growing day by day. So, in the years to come we should have larger production of apple juice.

For its preparation, apples are washed with a weak solution of acid to remove dirt, spray residues etc. and then crushed in a vessel to get the juice. It is filtered through a coarse cloth and heated to 82-85°, filled into clean bottles and then cooled.

Citrus Juices

During the season of citrus fruits, their juice is extracted, acidified with citric acid and preserved with potassium metabisulphite. The juice is filled in the suitable containers. Citrus fruits juice is full of vitamin C. So its demand is a bit higher than other juices.

Grape Juice

Coloured as well as white grapes can be used for making grape juice. Juice is extracted from the crushed grapes by means of a basket press. The extracted juice after filtration is bottled and when orgol or tartar settles down during storage, it is filtered again. Now, the clear juice is bottled and preserved by pasteurization or by addition of sodium benzoate.

Pineapple Juice

It is one of the most popular juices which is liked by people from all walks of life. Pineapple is peeled and its juice extracted through secrew type juicer. The juice is quickly heated to 88°, held at that temperature for 2-3 minutes and immediately filled into clean and steam cans, which are closed, inverted for a minute or two and then cooled. Canned pineapple juice could be stored for a period of 12-15 months without any serious loss in quality or nutritive value.

Similarly, mango, pomegranate and jamun juices are prepared by adding citric, ascorbic acids and some water to their juice and pulp as mentioned in the book. Fruit juices, sherbet, murabba, jam, jelly always contain potassium metabisulphite and citric acid (sometimes ascorbic acid is also added and in salty preparations, sod. benzoate and acetic acid are also added). Now, fruit juices are prepared to cater to the health needs and are better known as health drinks. Of late, some pharmaceutical companies are busy in making available specific disease-curing fruit juices in the market.

Natural Health Tips

1. Is Your Blood Red Enough?

A recent Health Ministry study shows that over a lakh Indian women die each year due to anaemia. Few tips on how to improve your energy levels are described here. In the third world, where female nutrition levels remain low, anaemia is one of the main causes of fatigue among women. In India, an estimated 83 per cent of the adult female population would qualify as anaemic. Anaemia or iron deficiency means that the blood does not have enough haemoglobin, the oxygen-carrying iron compound that gives human blood its characteristic red colour. With reduced oxygen availability, the body is unable to burn off sugar to produce needed energy.

An unbalanced and low-iron diet depletes iron reserves as does the consumption of devitalised refined foods and overprocessed foods lacking in life-giving ingredients. Iron may have nothing to do with energy production directly, but it is a mineral crucial to the transport of nutrients and oxygen as it is one of the chief components of the haemoglobin molecule. Iron is difficult to absorb—a person can absorb no more than 2 mg a day.

Iron deficiency is generally found among young women with menstrual problems and among those who have been continuing with a faulty diet for some months. Heavy blood loss due to serious injury, or ailments such as piles and heavy menstruation can also lead to anaemia. Even normal periods drain iron, pregnancies sap it, and weight-reducing diets cut down its intake.

Anaemia can also be a result of sustained emotional strain and anxiety, which affect the production of hydrochloric acid essential for the assimilation of proteins and iron. Again, a variety of drugs, such as aspirin and steroids, if taken in excess, can destroy beneficial intestinal flora, which, in turn, hampers the assimilation of certain vital vitamins and minerals, including iron. Vitamin E, especially, is very sensitive to the effect of drugs, and the absence of this vitamin leads to poor blood quality.

The normal level of haemoglobin in a person is 15 gm per 100 cc of blood. Since haemoglobin is the oxygen carrier of the body, its presence in adequate proportion is vital for respiratory and metabolic efficiency. Lack of haemoglobin can make you look haggard and can also lead to premature wrinkles. The absence of a vital blood ingredient like haemoglobin also results in slow clotting and in slow healing of wounds, weak eyesight, poor memory, general body weakness, frequent dizziness, fatigue, shortness of breath on exertion, headache, and depression.

Except in the case of heavy bleeding, anaemia doesn't come about overnight. To overcome it, supplements are essential and so is a proper diet.

- Common food rich in natural organic iron are wheat, brown rice (rice with husk), green leafy vegetables, cabbage, carrot, beet, tomatoes, and spinach. Apples, being rich in iron, arsenic and phosphorus are recommended. Other fruits rich in iron are bananas, grapes, dates and peaches.
- A small but essential amount of copper contained in apricots and almonds acts along with iron and vitamins as a catalyst in the synthesis of haemoglobin. Copper also boosts iron absorption.
- Supplements of trace elements, Vitamins B_{12} and folic acid are necessary for the proper production of haemoglobin. Folic acid deserves a special mention. In a study in which women received either iron alone, or folate alone, or iron and folate together, only 26 per cent of those who received a single nutrient showed a rise in haemoglobin.
- Foods like mangoes, raisins, red beets, spinach and lettuce supply a good form of vegetable haemoglobin.

- One cup of freshly-sprouted moong seeds, taken early morning on an empty stomach, also helps. Alternatively, make an emulsion of black sesame seeds by grinding them and adding water. To this, add just a dash of milk and jaggery. Take half a cup on an empty stomach every day.
- Though many naturopaths ask anaemics to eschew fasting, microscopic examination of blood before and after fasting has shown an overall improvement in the quality of blood after fasting.
- Ayurveda offers the most comprehensive cure for anaemia. Special ayurvedic iron preparations are humanised, non-toxic iron oxides, prepared by repeated incineration of iron, as well as by cooking it in various herbal substances. As iron supplements weaken the digestion, they should be taken with compensating herbs, such as ginger and cinnamon to improve digestion. Good formulas are the famous shatavari and the ashwagandha compound. Chyavanprash has also been used for curing anaemia for thousands of years.
- Two glasses of carrot and spinach (palak) juice in the ratio of 3:1 every day with breakfast are good for anaemics.

2. Plugging Diet Deficiencies

Naturopathy emphasizes the role of diet for prevention and cure of a wide range of health problems. To function optimally, the body needs a balanced proportion and quantity of the right types of foods. When this does not happen, nutritional deficiencies lead to many illnesses and disorders.

The five types of nutrients essential for sustaining health include (1) carbohydrates (2) proteins (3) fats (4) vitamins and (5) minerals. Unfortunately, our fast-paced lifestyles do not ensure that we get the requisite daily intake of all essential nutrients. Regular meals are often skipped, or replaced by aerated drinks, fat-foods, and endless cups of coffee. Over a period of time this causes nutritional deficiencies. Think of these deficiencies as bullets targeting a cardboard cutout. For a while, the cutout will remain standing, but as the bullet holes become more numerous and bullets attack more vulnerable areas, the cutout will collapse. So will the human body.

Fortunately, nature has provided a unique food that has the total complement of nutrients you need to safeguard against nutritional deficiencies: Spirulina. This micro alga has been called the "most powerful food on earth" because it has vast quantities of protein, vitamins, minerals and trace elements, in addition to 18 to 22 amino acids you need. Since the taste of spirulina does not appeal to all palates, it may be safely taken in capsule or tablet form. Just 2 capsules daily will put something EXTRA back into your life-for life.

3. Prevent Stress, Naturally

Everyone has problems. Everyone faces failure or losses. The difference is that while some cope well with challenges and tensions, others are overwhelmed. The result: STRESS. Stress can be a temporary phenomenon, or a continuing one. Its outcome is more harmful when it is unrelenting and left unmanaged. Stress can strain relationships and affect your performance as a parent, a husband, a professional.

In the short-term, stress can lead to physical symptoms of insomnia, loss of appetite, fatigue, irritability, anxiety attacks, or breathlessness. In the long-term, stress can cause hypertension or high blood pressure with its attendant health problems—like a higher predisposition to heart attacks and strokes. In India, it is estimated that as many as 20-30% of urban adults have hypertension.

How can one manage stress? Yoga, regular exercise, music, a hot bath, a drink or two, sharing the problem with a friend—these can certainly help. But, is there a solution for those who do not have these options?

Fortunately, nature has provided us with a herb that has amazing properties: The root of the herb Ashwagandha (Withania somnifera) has proven extremely efficacious in restoring the body's natural ability to cope with stress and perform optimally. Herbal supplements containing extract of ashwagandha are safe and without side-effects. They rejuvenate you and enable you to cope with problems before they get the better of you. However, if the problem remains, it is advised that you seek professional help.

4. Healthy Diet Prevents Cancer

It is said that vitamins A, C, E, fibre diet, fruits and vegetables play an important role in keeping the human system free of the dreaded cancer disease. On the contrary, consumption of alcohol and fried foods could cause cancer of liver and stomach, and tobacco is the number one enemy of the human race. Its consumption in any form like smoking or chewing causes lung and throat cancer.

Recent statistics released by the World Health Organisation have revealed that 38 million people in the US have quitted smoking tobacco. But in India, it is increasing. This results in around 3,000 deaths everyday.

It is pointed out that 90 per cent of cancer cases are curable if detected at an early stage. The emphasis should also be on prevention through education and cure by detection at an early stage. Help the patients by referring them to rehabilitation centres and conduct surveys and prepare strategies to further combat cancer, not only in rural areas but in cities as well. Not much is known about cancer. Unlike other diseases cancer does not give early symptoms.

5. Healthy Diet for Healthy Heart

A diet rich in fruits and vegetables and low in meat and sugar can not only help lower blood pressure but also can reduce levels of homocysteine, a compound linked with heart disease, researchers have said. They said a new study showed that a healthy diet can affect the heart and circulatory system in more than one way.

The diet, known as dietary approach to stop hypertension (DASH), includes plenty of fruits and vegetables. Only low-fat dairy foods are allowed and meat and sugar are cut back.

Regular intake of this diet showed that it helped significantly in lowering the blood pressure. Some researchers also checked that the effect of DASH was on homocysteine, an amino acid linked with heart disease that is produced by metabolising protein. Results show that modifying the diet can have multiple benefits, behind changes in traditional risk factors such as blood pressure and cholesterol. To get these benefits, people should eat a well-balanced diet. It is not enough to eat just an occasional fruit or vegetable while consuming a high-fat diet, but regular intake is essential. The researchers came up with the DASH diet consisting of fruits & vegetables after learning that vegetarians had a lower risk of heart disease.

6. Is Raw Food the Secret of Staying Young?

If you really want to eat healthy food, disconnect your oven. The latest trend among the dedicatedly health-conscious people is to eat only raw food because the theory goes that it is the "natural" way we are designed to eat.

Raw-food advocates believe that many common health disorders can be traced to our taking the wrong nutritional track a few centuries back. Our ancestors lived exclusively on raw food and lived for much longer years than us. Those interested in eating raw food, believe that it is also the key to staying young. After eating mainly raw foods for seven years and a completely raw diet for the past two years, one feels like a new person, physically and mentally. It's like de-ageing.

Eating raw foods provides you with a cocktail of essential vitamins, minerals, amino acids, antioxidants, enzymes and phytochemicals that work together to promote your health, says Patrick Holford, author of the *Optimum Nutrition Bible.* But once a food is heated, he says, essential enzymes are destroyed, which means that the body is unable to digest it properly and extract nutrients from it.

Switching to a raw plant-food diet also improves your memory, helps you think clearly and cleanse the body by removing the toxins. It increases energy levels, says nutritionist Rozalind Gruben.

Food is for pleasure as well as health. Certain compounds such as carotenoids (found in orangey-yellow vegetables) and lycopene (a powerful antioxidant with anticancer properties, found in tomatoes), are made more accessible through cooking.

It just takes three months to help heal digestion and improve overall health.

7. How Many Calories do We Really Need?

How many calories per day does an ordinary person need? In India, the norm is supposed to be 2,400 calories in rural areas and 2,200 in urban areas. The official poverty line is linked to rural and urban incomes corresponding to this level of calorie intake in 1973. According to official thinking, if you consume less than this level of calories, you are suffering from malnutrition.

I think it is high time we challenged these norms and came up with better ones. We tend to take for granted whatever we are told by nutritionists.

Few of us have the time or inclination to try and estimate how many calories we actually consume. But recently an advertisement by an American fast food chain called Subway, says something different.

Subway specialises in what are called submarine sandwiches cylindrical rolls of bread stuffed with meat and vegetables. Subway prides itself on providing low-calorie sandwiches in contrast to high-calorie hamburgers sold by multinational chains like McDonalds and Burger King.

A six-inch Subway sandwich with turkey-breast and ham has only 288 calories, the advertisement boasts. Even a Subway club sandwich has no more than 312 calories. The count will go up if you add cheese or mayonnaise. But the basic calorie count is low.

By contrast, the Big Mac, the best-selling burger of McDonalds, contains 560 calories. And the Whopper, the best-selling sandwich of Burger King, contains 660 calories. So, says Subway, eat our submarine sandwiches and keep the weight down.

We are not greatly concerned with the rival claims of these fast-food chains. What concern us in the light of these figures are the nutritional norms. The advertisement looks accurate, it quotes the websites of McDonalds and Burger King as its data source. From this it follows that if you eat a turkey and ham Subway sandwich for breakfast, a Big Mac for lunch and a

Whopper for dinner, then your total daily intake will add upto just 1,508 calories. So, going by Indian nutritional norms, eating such junk food will leave you severely under-nourished!

Now, all these years we have been under the impression that Americans are overweight precisely because they stuff themselves with Big Macs and Whoppers. A Big Mac is a double-decker sandwich, with two meat cutlets, cheese, tomato and lettuce wedged between three layers of bread. A Whopper boasts that it has even more meat than a Big Mac. Both are fatty. A Big Mac has 35 grams of fat, a Whopper 40 grams would be a recipe for obesity, I had always thought. But according to our nutritional norms, this is a recipe for under-nourishment.

Surely we need to take a searching look at these norms, as going by an FAO norm, two-thirds of all Americans were under-nourished. I wondered then whether nutritionists tended to exaggerate calorie requirements to increase their importance and gain more publicity than Subway advertisements.

There are other straws in the wind. In India, the poverty line in 1973 was based on income levels corresponding to 2,400 calories and 2,200 calories respectively in rural and urban areas. But subsequently the calorie intake has been falling in virtually every income group, from top to bottom. Originally, the poverty line was supposed to represent the level below which people were hungry. But in the 1993 National Sample Survey, over 36 per cent of people fell below the poverty line whereas only 8 per cent failed to get two square meals a day. The poverty line and hunger line have diverged widely in the last three decades.

One possible explanation is that increased mechanisation has reduced calorie needs. Even in rural areas bus services have increased greatly and the use of cycles and motor-cycles has reduced walking time.

Tractors, combined harvesters, dehusking machines, milling machines and other such devices have greatly reduced the physical labour involved in agriculture.

Even in urban areas, mechanisation (washing machines, pressure cookers, motorised transport) has reduced the need for physical effort. It is rightly said that there are large variations in calorie requirements from person to person.

Indeed, the notion of a standard calorie norm for all human beings ignores the way the body adapts to external circumstances. Many studies show that more food in early years translates into greater height, and tall persons need more food. By the same token, less food in one's early years can translate into shorter human beings, who need fewer calories. A person who is 5 ft. tall needs fewer calories than one who is 6 ft. tall.

But if you assume that all people need the same amount of calories, you will regard short persons as underfed even though their bellies may in fact be full. A standardised calorie norm for all human beings is a recipe for exaggerating malnutrition. So, a fresh look to this is needed by nutritionists exclusively at this stage.

8. Do You Get More Colds than Your Friends?

Although the range can vary widely, an average adult suffers about two to four colds a year. Women, especially those between the age of 20 and 30, have more colds than men. One of the reasons for this, say experts, might be their closer contact with children who frequently suffer from colds. This seems to be related to youngsters' relative lack of resistance to infection and to contacts with other children in creches and schools. Children have about six to eight colds a year. But sometimes, the number of colds per child can even be as high as 10 a year, say experts. But it seems that your colds tend to go down as you grow older. Studies have shown that on an average, people above the age of 60 have fewer than one cold a year.

9. Why is Spice Nice?

Spices and herbs are good not only for your taste buds but also for your health. They can supply calcium, iron, vitamin B, carotene, vitamin C and other antioxidants in small amounts. For instance, fresh parsley has been linked with cancer prevention due to its antioxidant content. Spicy food is much more appealing than a vitamin pill. Besides, herbs and spices don't have any kilojules or fat, so you can eat them to your heart's content, or till your tongue allows you to!

10. Why are Anti-oxidants Useful?

Oxidation is when high levels of oxygen react with exposed surfaces. It happens every time you take in a breath of air. This process has by-products called free radicals. These are unstable oxygen molecules which react with normal healthy body cells and damage them. This repetitive damage leads to degenerative diseases like cancer, heart trouble, diabetes, arthritis, cataract and ageing etc.

Free radical production is increased by pollution, physical and mental stress, contaminants, as well as by common vices like smoking.

However, this damage and the resultant diseases can be prevented. You have to only make sure that you get enough anti-oxidants, which as per studies, counter the damages caused by naturally occurring oxygen molecules known as free radicals.

Anti-oxidants are beneficial compounds that neutralize free radicals before they can attack your body cells. Your diet (carrots, tomatoes, other yellow and orange fruits and green vegetables) does give you anti-oxidants, but not enough.

People could have lived longer and be healthier if they took daily supplement of vitamin C, E, beta-carotene (life-booster vitamins) as explored by scientists in USA Department of Agriculture, Human Nutrition Research Centre on Aging.

These vitamins are called anti-oxidants for fruits and vegetables and are better & safer to reduce risk of said diseases and problems.

- A healthy adult should take:

  250-1000 mg of Vitamin C or 15 oranges.

  100-400 I.U. Vitamin E or 1/2 cup to 2 cups of sunflower.

  17000-50000 I.U. of beta-carotene or 5 carrots.

- Natural beta-carotene is also available in high dozes. It comes from the micro-algae **Dunaliella salina,** and the yellow pigment found in fruits and vegetables. Beta-carotene is one of the nature's best anti-oxidants. Just one softgel gives you 10 mg of natural beta-carotene, which is equal to 5 servings of fruits and 5 servings of vegetables enough to let you forget about some of your biggest potential health problems.

- Daily doses of 53 foods could extend your life and may help neutralize body oxidation reactions producing free radicals linked to various diseases including cancer and Alzheimer's. Research continues to find evidence that many ailments are linked as said above with free radicals. At the same-time, there is evidence that we can help prevent or even treat these diseases with the following diet rich in four key anti-oxidants:

  (a) Apricot, Asparagus, Cantaloupe, Carrots, Coriander, Mango, Papaya, Peaches, Pumpkin, Spinach, Sweet Potatoes, Tomatoes, Watermelon.

  (b) ***Foods high in vitamin C*** – Cabbage, Cantaloupe, Capsicum, Cauliflower, Proccoli, Chillies, Gooseberry, Guava, Grapefruit, Lemons, Mango, Orange, Strawberries, Tomatoes, Turnip, Amla, Papaya.

  (c) ***Foods high in vitamin E*** – Almonds, Sunflower oil, Corn oil, Sunflower seeds, Wheat-germ oil, Olive oil, Raw wheat germ, carrots' green leaves.

  (d) ***Foods high in selenium*** – Barley, Brown rice, Cabbage, Carrots, Celery, Lentils (Dab), Molasses, Mushrooms, Onions, Garlic, Red meats, Seafood, Soyabean, Spinach, Wheat flour, Wheat germ.

11. Role of Vitamins/Minerals in Our Body

(a) ***Calcium*** – Essential for bone/teeth and maintains bone density & strength. Helps regulate heart-beat, muscle contractions, nerve function, and blood clotting. May help prevent hypertension. Adequate calcium helps prevent or minimize osteoporosis. Vitamin D and lactose help improve calcium absorption. Oxalic acid found in spinach may reduce calcium absorption. Too much of it causes kidney damage, constipation, nausea, excessive thirst, abdominal pain and general confusion.

Source: Milk products and fruits. Dosage 500 mg/day.

(b) ***Iron*** – Essential for haemoglobin which carries oxygen into blood and myoiglobin (in muscle). Forms part of several enzymes and proteins in our body. Vitamin C helps in better iron absorption. Too much of it causes nausea, abdominal pain, constipation and a damage to liver & heart.

Source: Fruits & green vegetables.

(c) ***Copper*** – Helps in formation of R.B.C. and keeps total system healthy.

Source: Beans, nuts, potatoes.

(d) ***Iodine*** – Necessary for thyroid gland function and normal cell metabolism.

Source: Sea food, sea weed, iodised salt.

(e) ***Zinc*** – Important for active enzymes needed for cell division, growth and repair (wound healing) for immune system, taste and smell. Promotes growth & sexual maturity, helps digestion of fruits. Too much of it causes vomiting, diarrhoea & damage to kidneys.

Source: Fish, sea food, fruits – sharifa & naspati.

(f) ***Magnesium*** – Aids in bone growth, basic metabolic functions, nerves & muscles including heart muscle (important for heart).

Source: Banana, whole grain, vegetables, milk.

(g) ***Phosphorus*** – Helps build bone and teeth & form cell membrane and genetic material. Vital for energy production.

Source: All foods.

(h) ***Selenium*** – Part of enzymes that act as anti-oxidants that prevent cell damage by oxygen-derived compounds and thus protects against cancer. Needed for proper immune system.

Source: Garlic, fish, sea food.

(i) ***Vitamin C*** – Helps bones, teeth and connective tissues to form, strengthens blood vessel wall, helps wound heal faster. Too much of it interferes with the action of, contraceptive pill. It is also an anti-oxidant vitamin like vitamin E.

Source: Citrus fruits, Amla.

(j) **Vitamin A** – Helps clear vision, maintains healthy skin and mucous membranes, assists growth and production. Too much of it may cause birth defects. Its deficiency may cause problems like headache, peeling skin, loss of hair, cracked lips, blurred vision, vomiting & loss of appetite. It also acts as an anti-oxidant like beta-carotene.

Source: Fish, carrot, yellow fruits.

12. Nature's Remedy for Hypertension

Hypertension or high blood pressure can lead to serious health disorders and must not be neglected. Lifestyle changes like weight loss, avoidance of salt, and increased intake of fruits and vegetables can help bring down blood pressure in most people, but they would need to maintain these changes permanently in order to maintain control over blood pressure. Vegetarian diets are reported to significantly lower the blood pressure. Some doctors also recommend cutting back on sugar intake. The combination of hypertension and smoking greatly increases the risk of heart disease-related sickness and death. Many studies have also found a relationship between alcohol consumption and blood pressure. Stress in men has been linked to eventual hypertension.

Daily exercise can lower the blood pressure significantly. Obese people are prone to blood pressure. Weight loss in consultation with a specialist is recommended for those who are both overweight and hypertensive. Nutritional supplements made from ashwagandha can reduce stress, and the herb garlic can bring down blood pressure. Garlic (Lahsun) has heating and drying properties. It is an excellent stimulant, carminative and expectorant. Its juice is a disinfectant, rejuvenative and antispasmodic. Garlic has a rejuvenating effect on all tissues and symptoms and has been seen to lower the blood pressure safely and significantly. In many clinical trials, garlic has also been found effective in relieving joint problems and arthritis. It is beneficial for diabetic and cancer patients. Garlic cloves can be chewed, cooked, powdered, taken as tea, a decoction, infusion, in food and as an infused oil. Consult a physician before consuming large quantities of garlic, and if hypertension persists.

13. Ease the Ulcer, Banish the Cough

Licorice is widely used as a flavouring agent in confectionery, and as a key ingredient in many medicines. Known as mulethi in India, it has been used in Ayurveda for hundreds of years for its therapeutic properties to treat throat and respiratory problems and to soothe rashes and infections. Most throat lozenges contain mulethi in conjunction with other beneficial herbs like pepper, laung, methi or adrak.

The sweet-tasting root of licorice is, indeed, a popular healing herb. It is an astringent, a demulcent, expectorant and germicide with laxative and alterative properties. It also has anti-inflammatory and anti-arthritic properties and is widely used to treat muscle and joint problems. Mulethi is also an antibacterial and antiviral.

What is less known, perhaps, is that mulethi strengthens the nerves, promotes the memory, treats digestive disorders, and disorders of the spleen and liver, constipation, gastritis, and above all, prevents and treats ulcers. If traditional time-tested usage is not enough to convince you of the therapeutic properties of this remarkable herb, it may help you to know that the herb's efficacy has been demonstrated in many clinicial studies and German scientists have officially approved licorice as an ulcer treatment. Licorice contains several anti-ulcer compounds that work to protect the digestive lining from aspirin's ulcer promoting effect. In fact, mulethi is more effective in speeding ulcer healing than pharmaceutical drugs.

Add a little licorice to your tea to make a home remedy, or buy any of the remedies available in the market. Long-term daily usage of mulethi beyond six weeks is not recommended.

14. Eat Your Boron

If you're skimping on your apples, bananas, oranges and other fruits, you could be short-changing your brain. In a study, when 15 people ate combinations of chicken, mashed potatoes, rice, skim milk and bread, but did without most fruits and vegetables for two months, tests showed that their brains were low in a nutrient called boron. In tests of memory, perception and attention, researchers found that the low-boron brain performed less than the brain recharged with the nutrient. And measurements of brain activity showed low-boron state to be closer to drowsiness than to alertness. Boron may affect the permeability of brain cells, helping them to more rapidly transmit information, explains the study conducted by the author James G. Penland, Ph.D., a research psychologist at the USDA Human Nutrition Research Centre. It took a 3-milligram supplement of the nutrient to bring the participants' brainpower upto good level.

15. Eye-Saver: Not Carrot, But Spinach

The most common cause of blindness in the elderly people may be prevented by eating right kind of food according to a new study. And despite what your mother told you, spinach, not carrots, appears to help your eyes the most.

Macular degeneration generally hits people in their sixties. It begins when the macula — part of the retina — thins as cells die off. Vision area begins to leak; if untreated, this can result in blindness within weeks. Scientists have speculated that the damage might be the handiwork of oxygen molecules called free radicals, and that anti-oxidants, which collar free radicals before they can do harm, could help.

Ophthalmologist Johanna Seddon, at the Massachusetts Eye and Ear Infirmary, with the help of researchers at five other major eye centers, tested this theory by asking 876 patients — 326 of whom suffered from macular degeneration — to fill out a detailed questionnaire on what they regularly ate. Seddon found that people who ate antioxidant-rich fruits and vegetables at least five times a week, had about half the risk than those who avoided these foods. When she looked at which foods were most responsible for the protective effect, spinach and collard greens stood out. Interestingly, taking antioxidant-vitamin pills such as A and E give no advantage. Seddon thinks two antioxidants plentiful in leafy greens — lutein and zeaxanthin — supplied the boost. The eye contains both nutrients, and they seem to help block out blue light, which damages the retina.

"Eating spinach more than once in a week was enough to lower the risk", Seddon says, "and the effect got stronger, more the subjects ate."

16. Low Cancer Risk with Meatless Diet

While some meat-eaters still believe that vegetarianism is an unhealthy fad, a major British study has established that vegetarians have a 40 per cent lower risk of dying from cancer, compared to meat-eaters. This is the first study to investigate the correlation between a vegetarian diet and cancer risk.

The study observed a large group of 11,000 people — 5,000 of them vegetarian — over a period of eleven years. The researchers found that the vegetarians had a 20 per cent lower risk of dying of any cause and a 40 per cent lower risk of losing their lives to cancer or heart disease.

The study was published in the British Medical Journal and carried out by the London School of Hygiene and University of Oxford. However, the head of the research team felt that there is not sufficient cause to give up meat totally. Also, a vegetarian diet may be deficient in certain minerals and proteins, which must be made up with supplements.

17. Tossing Tomatoes at Cancer

Nutrition nags are always warning us that vitamin pills can't substitute for a healthy diet. But busy people struggling to find time for all those balanced meals might wonder what we get from fruits and vegetables can't be found in a pill. Chemists at Cornell University have a partial answer. They've isolated two substances in tomatoes that may help prevent cancer.

In a quest for compounds that block the body's formation of potent carcinogens (cancer-causing substances) called nitrosamines, food chemist Joseph Hotchkiss whirled up a batch of tomato juice. He knew that vitamin C in tomatoes can keep nitrosamine levels low, but an earlier experiment made him suspect that something else was going on as well. In that study, 16 tomato-eating volunteers cut their nitrosamine levels beyond what would be expected from their vitamin C intake alone.

To pin down the compounds responsible, Hotchkiss and colleague Michael Helser mixed tomato extracts with chemicals that normally combine to form nitrosamines. Two of the substances isolated from tomatoes were winners: P-coumaric acid and chlorogenic acid — each cut the amount of nitrosamines formed by about 20 per cent.

Hotchkiss's earlier study indicated that P-coumaric acid and chlorogenic acid may also be present in other produces, including capsicums, strawberries and carrots. The acids are part of a larger class of chemicals called phenols, many of which have shown promise as cancer-fighters.

18. Fruit Smoothies for Skin

Something that "eats" skin sounds pretty scary, but in fact it may be the gentlest approach to facial exfoliating. Skincare products are now being formulated with enzymes from fruits like papaya and pineapple that digest the protein material which comprises the skin's outer layer, instantly rendering skin softer and smoother, says Mark Rubin, clinical instructor of dermatology at the University of California, San Diego. And though the same effects can also be achieved mechanically with a facial scrub, or chemically with alpha-hydroxy acids (AHAs) which dissolve the "glue" that binds dead skin cells, enzymes are a non-abrasive alternative particularly well suited for sensitive skin.

The anti-aging downside to enzymes is that they don't appear to yield any stimulating effects on the cells that produce collagen, the material that gives skin structural support. Still, when skin is extremely sub-damaged, enzymes help clear the way for penetration of such remedies as Retin-A (which is known to spur collagen) or AHAs (which are believed to). Furthermore, enzyme-enriched products are being used both pre-and post-peel, initially to help produce a more even "burn" and then afterward to minimize the flakiness that can last several days to several weeks, depending on the strength of the peel.

19. Food for Thought

Some of you may recall waking up in the mornings before school to a diet of soaked almonds prepared with brahmi leaves, before you partook of your breakfast—it's nourishment for the brain, you would be told if you protested. It will help your memory. And, you took it, if only to please your loving grandma.

Brahmi is now being hailed around the world. The National Geographic magazine did a special feature on prominent medicinal herbs, and brahmi (L. Baccopa monnieri) was among the select list. In ancient times it was noted that brahmi aided longevity and proved beneficial for skin diseases. Later research showed that apart from being a rejuvenating tonic, it neutralizes blood acids, and stimulates the central nervous system.

This inconspicuous creeping marsh plant can be found in gardens and in the wild. The bitter leaves contain chemical compounds called bacosides which strengthen or restore the ability of neurons in the brain that support learning and recall, improve alertness and relieve mental fatigue. Research has also demonstrated the role of other nutrients like vitamins B_1, B_6, B_{12}, and C, choline, folate, niacin, calcium, copper, iodine, iron, magnesium, manganese, potassium, zinc and lecithin—all of which seem related to memory. So, if you suffer from forgetfulness, make sure your diet has adequate quantities of these.

Take brahmi regularly. Apart from home remedies, you can buy brahmi formulations to boost the memory power. Remember to take brahmi regularly.

20. A Plate of Protection

Evidence continues to mount about the role of vitamins and minerals in good health. A new first-time study reported in the journal of the National Cancer Institute suggests that they may be protective against cancers of the digestive tract.

Researchers uncovered this finding after supplementing the diets of 30,000 residents of Linxian, China, where stomach and esophageal cancer is about 100 times more likely than in the United States. These folks (aged 40 to 69) took either a placebo or different combinations of vitamins and minerals in high doses.

These included the familiar antioxidants — vitamin C, vitamin E and beta-carotene — as well as other potential cancer-fighting nutrients.

After five years of daily supplement-taking, those taking a beta-carotene, vitamin E and selenium combo saw their risk of death from cancer drop by 13 per cent (primarily due to the drop in digestive cancers) and the risk of death from all causes drop by 9 per cent. Researchers also discovered reductions in strokes but further study is needed to substantiate that preliminary finding.

"This offers an encouraging sign that supplementation may be beneficial against cancer", says William Blot, Ph.D., research investigator chief at the bio-statistics branch, National Cancer Institute. It should be kept in mind, however, that this population was already low in the nutrients tested.

The benefits noted, says Dr. Blot, may be due to the nutrients' antioxidant properties. That is, these vitamins and minerals may be able to subdue the free-radical molecules that do tumour-promoting damage to DNA. Although no benefits were found for vitamin C, researchers aren't ruling it out. It may be noted that it needs to be given earlier in life or for longer periods to work.

"Soon we may be able to make a recommendation about supplements, but what people can do right now is eat a diet that's rich in fruits and vegetables", says Dr. Blot. Remember, beta-carotene is plentiful in orange and yellow ones, as well as in dark green leafy vegetables (think carrots, mangoes, papayas); vitamin E can be found in grains, nuts and vegetable oils; and selenium is found in seafood.

21. Get that Blood Flowing

If you suffer frequent, unexplained headaches, you could be suffering from diminished blood flow to the brain. Improve the circulation of blood through the brain, and chances are that the headache will clear up. That's what the herb ginkgo biloba does most effectively.

The ginkgo biloba is a tree thought to have existed for over 200 million years. Researchers found that its leaves contained strong antioxidant flavones—making them capable of reversing the ageing of the brain.

Medical studies have found that the flavonoid glycosides in extract of ginkgo biloba improve blood flow and oxygen to all the organs in the body. Because they improve cerebral blood flow, they act effectively as a brain tonic, especially recommended for the elderly. Similarly, because flavonoid glycosides improve circulation, they also make ginkgo a premium natural remedy for dilating the arteries and hence providing relief to people suffering from reduced blood flow and oxygenation to the legs of peripheral vascular disease. Extract of ginkgo also helps maintain good blood flow to the retina, and is considered a good therapy for macular degeneration.

The ginkgo leaves contain very little of the active compounds — hence a standardised extract may mean processing 50 kgs of leaves to get 1 kg of extract. The suggested dose of ginkgo extract is 150-300 mg a day. More than this can cause diarrhoea, irritability, and restlessness. It is recommended that remedies made from standardised extracts are best bought from reputed manufacturers.

22. Nutrition Loss

Vegetables and fruits like spinach, cabbage, beans, carrots, oranges, musambis, etc. are high in vitamins like A, C and beta-carotene.

When you peel, or cut them, you remove their natural protective skin and expose them to oxygen in the air. This makes the vegetables and fruits lose their nutritive value. Which is why you should always peel or chop fruits and vegetables just before cooking or consuming them. Or else, keep them away from air.

23. Poisoning from Fresh Fruits & Vegetables

When unpasteurized apple juice sickened more than 50 Americans late in 1996, killing at least one child, it became frighteningly clear that hazards can lie in seemingly benign foods. The culprit in that episode was Escherichia Coli 0157:H7, a virulent strain of ordinary gut bacteria. Packing a toxin that can cause kidney failure and even death, this type of E. coli is one of the nastiest members of a rogue's gallery of disease-causing organisms, such as salmonella, cyclospora, and hepatitis A that you can pick up from fruits and vegetables.

Most of these germs are present in the dung of farm animals and can contaminate produce when it falls on fertilized soil or is handled by someone who didn't wash up. Fruits and vegetables seem to pose a smaller health risk than meat and eggs. Still, the danger is real and should prompt you to take simple precautions.

Cooking kills most bacteria, but unless you're prepared to steam your salad, you'll need to take other measures. Thoroughly rinse raw produce before eating. Studies show that this step can reduce bacterial infection ten to 100-fold, which may be enough to keep you from getting sick. Scrubbing can't hurt; however, there's little evidence that dilute solutions of bleach or other cleansers help, and they may leave unappetizing residues. Keep produce away from meat, poultry seafood, and eggs. And remember to wash the knife, cutting board — and your hands — when you move between those groups.

Unpasteurized juices call for particular care, because just a few bad apples can infect an entire batch. (Produce with a rind or high acid content seems to be relatively safe, but even orange juice has, on occasions, caused food poisoning). To keep any bacteria from multiplying, treat unsterilized juices like ice cream: Don't let them get warm.

24. Avoid Constipation

When was it that you had your last bowel movement? Constipation refers to unduly infrequent or irregular bowel movements, with difficulty, discomfort and sometimes pain. And if you are a chronic sufferer, you will readily agree that constipation can be bothersome. And anxiety about it can cause other physical and mental symptoms like fatigue, depression and nausea. It must not be neglected.

Constipation happens mostly to adults over 40, and is generally caused by lack of dietary fibre and liquid. So, you should have 20-35 gms of fibre — from whole grains, fruits and vegetables, and drink at least 6 glasses of fluid daily, and take regular exercise. Avoid foods that aggravate the situation, and eat slowly and smaller meals.

It is wise not to use chemical laxatives, enema, and other medications. Fortunately for us, there is another natural, safer option — a herbal remedy which includes senna seed pods or leaves. Senna has cathartic, antiseptic, antispasmodic, cholegogue and cleansing properties. This makes senna the most powerful herbal treatment, especially for chronic constipation. While its stimulating laxative action aids bowel movement, it also soothes and protects the intestines. Its use is considered absolutely effective and safe, except if you suffer from hemorrhoids.

To make a senna infusion at home, steep 3-4 pods in 4-5 tablespoons of cold water and take 1-2 tablespoons at a time. Or, simply buy one of the easily available herbal formulations containing senna from the marketplace.

25. Let's Take Vitamin 'C' if this Helps

Remember those studies where colds cleared up faster in sniffers who took vitamin C supplements? Well, hospital patients with bronchitis and pneumonia also recovered faster with a daily C supplement. It has been suggested in a new study reported in the International Journal of Vitamin and Nutrition Research. The dose was 200 milligrams, an amount you could get in about two cups of orange juice. Scientists don't know yet if these results will hold up in further research. One possible clue: In healthy immune cells — our bodies' infantry against infection — vitamin C is found in high concentrations.

Studies suggest that your diet has much effect on your vision & if you eat more spinach, broccoli, cabbage, carrot and peppers, you will help prevent cataracts and macular degeneration. Here also vitamin C plays a role as broccoli, cabbage and peppers are rich source of vitamin C.

26. Life-Extending Formulae

The fountain of youth, the age-old dream, may not be out of reach. Chinese medical researchers say that they have found herbal medicines effective in slowing down the inexorable process of ageing.

Dr. Shen Ziyin and his associates are putting traditional Chinese prescriptions for boosting the immune system through vigorous clinical tests and DNA research. Trained in Western medicine and a member of the Chinese Academy of Sciences, Shen has spent four decades on basic research integrating Chinese and Western medical theories.

Western scientists say the accelerated demise of T cells — the cells which regulate immunity and control the production of antibodies — is a key cause of ageing, but there is still no prescription for slowing down the process, Shen said.

Researchers have found that older people produce more T cells with a molecule known as FAS, or CD-95. Another molecule, known as a ligand, groups FAS molecules together and leads to a process in which a cell self-destructs. Shen said the only way known to decelerate the production of T cells with FAS is by slowing the whole body's metabolism through minimal calorie intake. Shen said ageing was not only a personal health issue but had a social and economic dimension. "To live long, one has to livewell."

More than ten per cent of China's 1-3 billion people are 60 years or older, and the number is forecast to rise to 400 million, or a quarter of the total population, by the middle of this century. In ancient Chinese medical classics "shen" — literally meaning "kidney" — refers to a system that regulates the body's metabolism. If the "shen" functions badly, the body's clockwork is thrown out of kilter. A patient, regardless of natural age, exhibits symptoms of backache, hair loss, weakness at the knees and low immunity, common to the elderly. Premature ageing is often found among middle-aged patients suffering from chronic illnesses, which could respond to treatment aimed at nurturing the "shen."

Shen hypothesised that the Chinese herbal elixirs for boosting the immune system could also slow down natural ageing. The research on ageing took a giant stride in the 1990s with the advance of modern DNA studies, Shen said. Risking over-simplification, he said Chinese medicine takes a holistic approach to diagnostics.

27. About Agremone Mexicana

Commonly known as prickly poppy, the agremone mexicana plant grows in the wild all over the country specially in the northern States like Punjab, Uttar Pradesh and Haryana. In Hindi, the plant is known as Bhatbhamt or Phararthgi Dhattura. In fact, the plant grows throughout the hotter parts of India along roadsides and waste places. The plant is even used by doctors as a cure for various ailments.

The flowers of this plant are yellow in colour and are similar to mustard flowers. The agremone seeds are similar in colour and size as the mustard seeds which makes adulteration easy. Mustard crop is cut during March. Seeds of agremone also mature during this period, and are likely to be harvested along with the mustard seeds.

However, while the seeds of the agremone plant produce a toxic compound, its roots are believed to be useful in guineaworm infestation, skin diseases, leprosy, constipation, malaria, colic and inflammations.

In fact, the Ayurvedic doctors say that the agremone leaves are useful in curing cough, wounds, ulcers and skin diseases. The latex is considered useful in jaundice, skin disease, leprosy, blisters, ulcers, conjunctivitis, inflammations, burning sensation and malaria.

Generally, Sangutharine, a toxic compound of this plant, is known to affect only the blood vessels in the heart or the liver. But sometimes it even affects capillaries (blood vessels) in the kidney which become porous resulting in total renal shutdown. The toxin starts affecting the capillaries in the heart making them more porous. The blood starts oozing out from the vessels making it difficult for the heart to beat. In fact, myocardial support is required in such patients. If not treated on time, this stage can prove fatal resulting in cardio-respiratory failure.

Sangutharine also attacks proteins, vitamins and calcium deposits in the body resulting in their acute shortage. So the patients have to be given large amounts of proteins and vitamin C and E tablets to cover the losses. Calcium dosages are also given to the patients.

The toxic compound also disturbs the carbohydrate metabolism in the body resulting in acute diarrhoea and fever.

The patients who are now being admitted to the hospitals are also showing large-scale skin pigmentation specially in the lower limbs. In such patients the adulterated oil has affected the capillaries below the skin. Due to the capillaries dysfunctioning, the skin pigment, melanin, is getting affected resulting in pigmentation.

28. Vegetable Helps

No single food removes the risk of cancer, but experts believe that consuming plant-based foods helps, because they are low in saturated fats (linked to an increased risk of cancer, heart and other diseases) and high in fibre content (believed to lower the risk of colon cancer). They are also the best sources of Phytochemicals — natural substances in fruits and vegetables that contribute to the colour and flavour of vegetables and also appear to prevent the formation of certain tumours.

One phytochemical widely publicised is the antioxidant beta-carotene. But researchers believe that other carotenoids such as lutein — found in spinach, kale and other green leafy vegetables — are more effective than beta-carotene.

Other phytochemicals that help prevent cancer are limonen and phenols, found in citrus fruits, allyl sulphides in garlic and onions, sulphoraphane, indoles and isothiocyanates in broccoli, cauliflower, and other cruciferous vegetables.

29. Plant Compounds even more Powerful than Vitamins

The most common term for these compounds, as a group, is phytochemicals — which means simply, plant chemicals. A more descriptive name might be phytomins (pronounced FIGHT-a-mins). That suggests they're related to vitamins, which are already known to be essential to human life. It's also an easy way to refer to an ever-growing list of compounds with tongue-twisting names like allyl sulphides, isothiocyanates, zeaxanthins, isothiocyanates phenolics, phytoestrogens, flavonoids, flavones, flavonols and the ever-popular flavonones.

Unlike vitamins, you won't necessarily fall over if you don't get your phytomins. If you consider dietary health to be a one-rupee coin then on the one side you have vitamins, minerals, proteins and other nutrients that prevent classic deficiency symptoms. On the flip side, you have compounds that have pharmacological properties. Are they essential? Says Pierson, "I'd say that without these compounds in the diet, you're opening the door to cellular damage and premature onset of ageing, disease, even death."

There's already a long list of identified phytomins, but given their potential, they could become household words in the next few years. So here's a quick look at some of the most promising ones, including how they work and, most important, how you can easily get more of them into your diet.

(a) ***Flavonoids*** – These compounds, numbering approximately 4,000, have been getting a lot of attention lately because they supposedly explain why those pate-gobbling, butter-loving, wine-guzzling Frenchmen do not have as high a death rate from heart disease as might be expected. Researchers used to think it was due to alcohol, but now they're saying it's the flavonoids present in grape skins. When allowed to steep, these skins impart their dark purple colour to wine, along with their powerful nutrients. These, in turn, keep blood cells from clotting and causing a heart attack. White wine and mixed drinks don't have as pronounced an effect.

But while the French may love their wine, they also eat lots of fruits and vegetables, and these are also full of flavonoids. Onions, green beans, apples, celery, and citrus fruit, (especially the peel and pulp) have the most, as do grape juice, green and black teas.

"This is a very important class of compounds," says Elliott Middleton, Jr. M.D., professor of medicine at the State University of New York. "There are no data yet on whether flavonoids could be as essential as diet and exercise in lowering heart-disease risk, but it may be that if we consume these compounds on a regular basis, we'll have a reduced likelihood of heart disease."

Indeed, Dutch scientists studied 805 men for five years and found that those eating the most of five essential flavonoids were 32 per cent less likely to die of heart disease. Their daily diets included four cups of tea, an apple (with skin) and about a quarter cup of onions. Likewise, in seven countries around the world where the flavonoid intake was high, the national rates of death from heart disease were correspondingly low.

Although preliminary studies with human kinds are mixed, these flavonoids might have cancer-fighting qualities as well. For instance, tea drinkers in China have lower rates of throat cancer.

"I do think the anti-cancer effects of flavonoids exist," says Michael Wargovich, Ph.D., a researcher at the M.D. Anderson Cancer Center in Houston, "but possibly only in synergy with a lot of other compounds that are present in the same fruits and vegetables."

(b) ***Carotenoids*** – The long-standing chief of this group of phytomins is beta-carotene. It's the most abundant carotenoid in the foods we eat and the one most efficiently converted to vitamin A. Plus, it's a powerful anti-oxidant, which means it counters cell damage that could lead to widespread cancer and heart disease.

But there are more than 600 other carotenoids, and research is proving that some of them have similar disease-fighting properties. For example, scientists recently found that people in northern Italy who ate seven or more servings of raw tomatoes every week had 60 per cent less chance of developing colon, rectal and stomach cancer than those who ate two servings or less. In fact, eating tomatoes may be more effective in reducing the risk of cancer than eating fruits or green vegetables.

Tomatoes are one of the few foods rich in a carotenoid called lycopene. And since it survives heating and processing, it's still present in tomato paste, sauce, juice, even ketchup and pizza. Other sources include watermelon, pink and red grapefruit, guava, and sweet red peppers.

Other carotenoids meriting study are canthaxanthin (we warned you this was going to get multi-syllabic) and lutein. The former is found in certain mushrooms and used as a food colouring in cheese. When it was fed to lab rats, they developed 65 per cent fewer cancers. The latter is found with beta-carotene in vegetables such as spinach. Besides possibly protecting against cataracts, it, too, is being investigated for potential cancer-fighting properties.

(c) ***Genistein, Daidzein and Saponins*** – No, this isn't some slick law firm from outer space. This trio can forcefully represent you in the battle against high cholesterol, and prostate and colon cancer.

All three of these phytomins are present in soyabeans.

Clare Hasiter, director of the Functional Foods for Health Programme at the University of Illinois, a unique programme exclusively focusing on the study of phytochemicals and their role in preventing disease, explains: "Genistein is structurally very similar to estradiol, one of the estrogens we normally produce. Now, we know that estrogen can promote tumour growth, but genistein, because it's so similar, binds up the receptor cells in tissues and blocks out the estradiol. At the same time, genistein inhibits growth of new blood vessels, which tumours need in order to grow. And that's the theory, anyway, as to why women who consume lots of soy products, as in Japan, have a much lower rate of breast cancer than, say, American women."

Meanwhile, more than 40 clinical studies have shown that saponins can lower blood cholesterol. They do it, says Pierson, by blocking sites in the intestines that take up cholesterol.

Some (relatively) painless ways to get soya products in your diet: Mix tofu (available at some health-food stores in India) into salads or toss some chunks of it onto your greens. Dice it up and add it to soups. Stir-fry it. Add it to your favourite noodles recipe or hide some inside your Kebabs. But be sure to get it into your diet somehow.

You'll never remember the names of all these nutrients, and fortunately, you don't have to. Here's our list of the foods that are either extremely high in one or rich in a number of different groups.

30. Eat Them

(i) Soyabeans

(ii) Garlic (always crush or slice cloves finely to release phytochemicals)

(iii) Onions (eat white, yellow and red for a variety of flavonoids)

(iv) Tomatoes — even in ketchup

(v) Citrus fruit (flavonoids cluster in the peel and white, pulpy parts)

(vi) Cabbage — wins every nutrition contest

(vii) Watermelon

(viii) Beans — kidney

(ix) Tea — green or black (use tea bags instead of loose leaves, and steam for 5 to 10 minutes)

Major Contenders – Virtually all greens, such as spinach, carrots, apples (leave the skin on), grapes, grape juice and red wine, cauliflower, sweet potatoes, and celery. An easy way of getting a hefty dose of phytomins is to make a simple stew crammed full of nutrient-rich vegetables. Beats spending the day gnawing up cauliflower florets.

31. Relax with Scents

Forget about the roses. It may be that the aroma of green apples is Mother Nature's most powerful tranquillizer, says Alan R. Hirsch, M.D., neurological director of the Smell & Taste Treatment & Research Foundation in Chicago.

According to Dr. Hirsch, a scent can have a tranquillizing effect on the brain. "We've noted that the scent of lavendar, for example, seems to increase alpha-wave function in the brain — the same kind of wave activity associated with states of relaxation," he explains.

On another level, a smell can relax you by bringing back the good old days. "It's called olfactory-evoked nostalgia, where a scent reduces anxiety by bringing back happy memories from a less-complicated time in your life." Scents that evoke this response vary from person to person depending on personal experiences.

32. Your Anti-cancer Food Pharmacy

What's responsible for the anti-cancer effect of fruits and vegetables? That's the question tantalizing scientists around the world, and phytochemicals — compounds in carrots, cabbage and other foods — may just be the answer. Thousands of phytochemicals are present in produce — so many that researchers have yet to identify and isolate all of them. Here are 14 general classes of phytochemicals that research has identified as possible cancer fighters — and foods you can find them in.

- Carotenoids — cruciferous vegetables like cabbage, cauliflower, broccoli, greens, carrots, tomatoes, pumpkin, melon, citrus fruits.
- Coumarins -- cucumbers, parsley.
- Flavonoids — soyabeans (including soy-based foods like tofu) and brinjals.
- Phenolic acids — cruciferous vegetables, greens, carrots, celery, parsley, tomatoes, brinjals, peppers, cucumbers, pumpkin, melon, soyabeans, citrus fruits.
- Glucarates — whole grains, cruciferous vegetables, citrus fruits, tomatoes, brinjals, peppers.
- Indoles — cruciferous vegetables.
- Lignans — soyabeans and soya products.
- Monoterpenes — garlic, cruciferous vegetables, citrus fruits, parsley, carrots, celery, cucumbers, parsnips, tomatoes, brinjals, peppers, fennel.
- Phthalides — carrots, celery, parsley, fennel.
- Phytates — soyabeans and soya products, whole grains.
- Polyacetylenes — carrots, fennel, celery, parsley.
- Sulfides — garlic, cruciferous vegetables, onions.
- Triterpenes — garlic, soyabeans, whole grains, cruciferous vegetables, celery, carrots, tomatoes, cucumbers, peppers, brinjals.

33. For Dental Health

(a) A crisp, juicy apple or other raw, crunchy fruits & vegetables. The fibre in them helps scrape away bacteria & plaque. Plus all that chewing action exercises the gums & ligaments around the teeth, which stimulates new blood flow to the area.

(b) Chillies — Adding the hot stuff to your food will make your mouth water. That excess saliva helps neutralize acids & clean your teeth. Chillies also contain a good amount of Vitamin C, a nutrient necessary for strong gums.

(c) Carrot — Studies suggest that people whose diets are high in beta-carotene, the nutrient found in carrots, mangoes & other fruits and vegetables, have a lower risk of oral cancer than people who have lower intake of the nutrient.

34. Vision Vitamins

Here's one more reason for increasing your carotenoid intake: It may decrease your risk of age-related macular degeneration (ARMD), a cause of blindness after age 50. ARMD sufferers have night blindness, or impaired ability to see in the dark, as well as a limited range of visual acuity. Vitamin A, which is derived from carotenoids, has been known for decades to reduce night blindness. But the link between ARMD and carotenoids has only recently been identified by J.M. Seddon, M.D., of the Massachusetts Eye and Ear infirmary, and others at five American ophthalmology centres.

Among nearly 900 people studied, those with the highest intake of carotenoid-rich vegetables, had a 43 per cent lower risk of developing ARMD than those with the lowest intake. In particular, a higher intake of spinach or collard greens substantially lowered the risk. Foods rich in vitamin C appeared to have a small effect as well. Vitamin supplements, on the other hand, didn't seem to help much.

35. Anti-Asthma Dieting

Asthma sufferers often struggle to breathe as their respiratory systems frantically fight off invading allergens, but eating the right foods may help. British researchers at the University of

Nottingham found that, of 2,633 asthmatics, those whose dietary magnesium intake was above the average 380 mg per day showed significantly improved lung function as well as reduced airway "hyper-reactivity" and wheezing. Low magnesium, the researchers suspect, may play a role in causing allergies and asthma in the first place. Dietary sources of magnesium include fresh green vegetables, cabbage, cauliflower, broccoli etc. unmilled wheat germ, soyabeans, milk, whole grains and nuts.

36. Mineral Boost

Did you know that if your body becomes deficient in the minerals like magnesium, calcium and potassium, you are more likely to suffer irregularities in your heartbeat? And if you have an excess of iron, but insufficient copper levels, this greatly increases your risk of a heart attack, especially after 50.

One in 10 people in Britain currently takes a multivitamin, but recent research from America suggests it's also time to begin taking minerals more seriously.

In theory, if you eat plenty of fresh foods, including fruits and vegetables, you are ingesting all the nutrients the body needs. But evidence is mounting that this is no longer the case. In 1940, two food scientists, Dr. McCance and Dr. Widdowson, were asked by the Medical Research Council to analyse the mineral content of UK-grown fruits and vegetables. In 1991, the duo conducted similar studies for the Ministry of Agriculture, Fisheries and Foods. Recently, David Thomas, a geologist-turned-nutritionist, did a comparative study of their figures. He found that calcium levels in broccoli had dropped by up to 75 per cent.

If these figures are correct, why are mineral levels becoming depleted? "Intensive farming methods during the past 50 years, plus acid rain and overuse of artificial fertilizers, have reduced the absorption of minerals, such as selenium and zinc into our fruits, vegetables and grains," says Thomas. "Mass-produced fertilisers generally contain only three minerals, but there are more than 36 known minerals, 21 of which are vital. If they're not in our soil, they're not going to make it into our foods. This imbalance is having a big impact on our health. Also, pesticides and pollutants such as lead accumulate in the body and prevent absorption of essential nutrients."

When Thomas began experimenting at his clinic by giving liquid minerals to his patients, he noticed improvements in a variety of conditions, including leg cramps, chronic fatigue, hyperactivity in children, migraines and, in some cases, autism. Since 1984, when the Finnish Government decreed that all fertilisers should contain selenium, sperm mobility (the ability of sperm to swim) in subfertile men has increased by 35 per cent, while instances of heart disease and prostate cancers have fallen. "During the 1970s before joining the EU, we imported huge amounts of Canadian wheat, which is rich in selenium, and consequently the daily intake averaged 70 micrograms," says Dr. Margaret Rayman of the University of Surrey.

37. Citric Sense

Lemons are good for the skin, aid digestion and now neurologists claim that its smell aids concentration. A study found that those who worked in a lemon-scented room, made fewer mistakes. The tangy fragrance stimulates the area in the brain region that controls both the sense of smell and the ability to concentrate.

38. The Rainbow Diet

Red is the colour that heralds the peak of summer with the arrival of luscious vine ripened tomatoes and juicy water melons. The pigment that saturates with colour called lycopene, is one of the most powerful antioxidants yet tested.

Tomatoes supply as much as 90 per cent of all the lycopene many of us get—which could explain why a diet abundant in them seems to protect against several forms of cancer. In one study, researchers at the Aviano Cancer Centre in Italy found that people who ate raw tomatoes at least seven times a week cut their risk of stomach, bladder colon cancers by half.

A recent Harvard University study found that men who ate four to seven servings of tomato-based foods a week—from pizza sauce to tomato juice—were 20 per cent less likely to develop prostate cancer than men who avoided tomatoes. Men who ate ten servings or more cut their risk nearly by half.

Red is the colour of pomegranates (anthocyanins again) and of fresh beets, which owe their particularly rich hue to an antioxidant called betacyanin.

Beet pigments may help suppress the growth of bacteria. In 1994 of more than 60 fruits and vegetables, researchers at the University of Mainz in Germany found that beets also contain some of the most powerful cancer-fighting agents around. Like anthocyanins, the pigments in beets are susceptible to pH—the reason a dash of lemon juice or vinegar brightens their colour.

Orange is the colour of carrots and yams, mangoes and papayas. Beta-carotene, the pigment responsible, gets its name from carrots, but even leafy green vegetables like spinach are packed with it (the green of chlorophyll masks beta-carotene's true colour). Researchers have identified more than 600 related substances, called carotenoids, in hues ranging from pale yellow to deep red. Most occur in combination in fruits and vegetables.

Carrots are still among the richest sources of beta-carotene—and researchers say there's plenty of reason to munch a bunch. In studies conducted by the US Department of Agriculture, volunteers who ate in the range of two to three carrots a day saw their cholesterol levels fall by an average of 11 per cent.

The higher the levels of beta-carotene in the bloodstream, other research suggests, the lower the risk of heart attacks.

In a Bigham and Women's Hospital and Harvard University study of 87,000 nurses, women who ate five or more servings of carrots a week had 68 per cent less risk of stroke than women who ate no more than one serving a month.

Yellow is the colour of corn and turmeric and of golden peppers. The pale yellow colour of potatoes and cauliflower comes from pigments called anthoxanthins (Greek for "yellow flower"), which function as antioxidants. The deeper hue of yellow peppers comes from beta-carotene.

Corn gets its colour from another antioxidant, called lutein, which plays a special role in preventing macular degeneration, one of the leading causes of blindness among older people. Lutein and its chemical cousin, zeaxanthin, are both found just behind the iris, where their colour helps protect the retina from potentially damaging light rays. A diet rich in both (including not only corn but also dark green vegetables like spinach) may significantly lower the risk of macular degeneration.

A very different pigment, called curcumin, saturates turmeric, the spice that gives curry powder its distinctive yellow—and may help lower the odds of cancer. In one study, rats fed curcumin and then exposed to cancer-causing chemicals developed fewer and smaller tumours than rats on a standard diet. Scientists at the Amala Cancer Research Centre in India have found in other animal studies that skin cancers treated with curcumin are less likely to spread to other parts of the body than untreated cancers.

Green is the colour of spinach and beans. Like the green of all plant life, it comes from chlorophyll, the only substance in nature that can collect and store energy from the sun.

Researchers now suspect that when chlorophyll is broken down during digestion, it becomes a potent defence against cancer. Animals fed a compound much like this digested chlorophyll and exposed to carcinogens show a significantly lower risk of developing cancers of the stomach, colon, and liver, according to Oregon State University researchers.

More amazing still, when mice are fed the green pigment and then exposed to a potent skin cancer causing substance, they develop far fewer tumours than untreated mice.

Experts say a single daily serving of spinach has enough chlorophyll to substantially cut the risk from many cancer-causing substances that may sneak into the diet. The darker the vegetable, the more chlorophyll it contains. So, go for the green.

Blue/Purple is the colour of concord Grapes, of course, deeply dyed wth the pigment anthocyanin ("blue flower" in Greek). In fact, there are many different forms of anthocyanins, with a palette that ranges from pale red to the deep purple of blackberries.

Anthocyanins show up in every thing from concord grapes and eggplants to radishes and red cabbage. The pigments are sensitive to pH—so in acidic conditions they tend towards red, in alkaline conditions towards the blue end of the spectrum. (A little baking powder, which is alkaline, can turn a deep red wine to pale blue-grey.) Anthocyanins are antioxidants, which may explain why laboratory experiments show they can neutralize several common carcinogens.

Surprisingly, anthocyanins also dilate blood vessels, which may help lower the risk of heart disease and stroke by keeping arteries open and flowing. Experts believe that the anthocyanins in grapes may be one reason that a glass of red wine at dinner helps lower the risk of heart attack.

39. Anti-oxidant: Anti-disease

On the surface, we all look healthy. You will see the starting point of some of the scariest diseases known to man — cancer, heart disease, diabetes, cataract and so many others. They all begin at the cell. They have a common name: 'degenerative', or age-related diseases. The process that causes them is going on inside your body.

(a) ***What Causes Degenerative Diseases?*** – The main cause of degenerative diseases is damage to healthy cells, mostly by oxidation.

(b) ***What is Oxidation?*** – Have you ever seen the cut portion of an apple turn brown? This reaction is called oxidation. It's also the process that your body uses to burn food for energy. It goes on inside your body, every time you breathe. But the rogue molecules called free radicals, can oxidise healthy cells, starting an oxidation chain reaction. One damaged cell produces more free radicals, which damage more cells. It leads to tissue damage and finally disease.

(c) ***Are You at Risk?*** – Our diet and lifestyles have changed. Most of our foods do not come from fresh source. They are all refined and packed foods.

Production of free radicals is increased by the exposure to air pollution, increased ultra violet radiation due to ozone layer depletion, and contaminants in food and water. Smoking, lack of sleep, unplanned diets and physical and mental stress also increase oxidation damage, and therefore the risk of degenerative diseases.

(d) ***Can Oxidation Damage be Stopped?*** – No, but it can be reduced dramatically. You can do this by adopting a healthy lifestyle, and you can also make sure you get enough anti-oxidants.

(e) ***What are Anti-oxidants?*** – Anti-oxidants are beneficial compounds that neutralise free radicals before they can attack healthy body cells. Examples of anti-oxidants are vitamin C, vitamin E, carotenoids and minerals such as zinc and selenium. They are part of your daily diet: fruits and vegetables are major sources. But to get enough you must eat 5 servings of fruits and 5 servings of vegetables.

(f) ***Just how Important are Anti-oxidants?*** – Across the world, anti-oxidant supplementation is being recognised as one of the most viable solutions to the health problems of modern, urban living. Doctors and researchers alike are recommending them for a longer, more healthy life.

(g) ***Is there a Practical Way to Get Enough Anti-oxidants?*** – It's not possible to eat enough fruits and vegetables everyday. The solution is natural beta carotene. It comes from the micro-algae Dunaliella salina. This is nature's richest source of carotenoids, which are, in turn, among the nature's best anti-oxidants. These are the yellow pigments found in yellow, orange, red and some green fruits and vegetables (carrots, oranges etc.). One soft gel capsule of natural beta carotene gives you 10 mg of mixed carotenoids, which is the same as the amount found in 5 servings of fruits and 5 servings of vegetables.

(h) ***Why Natural Beta Carotene?*** – Unlike synthetic beta carotene supplements now available in the market, natural beta carotene is a mixture of carotenoids similar to that found in fruits and vegetables. All these carotenoids work together to promote your health.

(i) ***How Exactly does Natural Beta Carotene Help?*** – Parry's natural beta carotene is a safe source of Vitamin

A (the body converts beta carotene of vitamin A as and when required). But more importantly it acts as a potent anti-oxidant, protecting you from the ravages of free radical damage, reducing the risk of degenerative diseases like: cancer, diabetes, heart disease, arthritis, stress reactions, cataract and other macular degeneration conditions.

40. Olive Oil

Olive oil may protect against colon cancer. According to recent report by British doctors, addition of olive oil to the list of foods may help prevent colon cancer. A new study by researchers at the University of Oxford adds to the growing body of evidence that shows olive oil, a staple of the Mediterranean diet, as good as fresh fruits and vegetables in keeping colon cancer at bay.

Dr. Michael Goldacre and a team of researchers at the Institute of Health Sciences compared cancer rates, diets and olive oil consumption in 28 countries including Europe, Britain, the US, Brazil, Columbia, Canada and China. Countries with a diet high in meat and low in vegetables had the highest rates of the disease and olive oil was associated with a decreased risk. "Olive oil may have a protective effect on the development of colon cancer," Goldacre said. Meat, fish and olive oil were the key elements of the diets in terms of cancer. Meat and fish combined were positively associated with the incidence of cancer but olive oil had a negative effect. The researchers believe that olive oil protects against bowel cancer by influencing the metabolism of the gut. They think it cuts the amount of a substance called deoxycyclic acid and regulates the enzyme diamine oxidase which may be linked to cell division in the bowel. Olive oil also:

- lowers bad cholesterol level
- reduces the risk of heart attack
- protects good cholesterol
- contains natural anti-oxidants which fight cell ageing.
- does not deteriorate during frying.

Comparative Chart of Olive Oil and other Vegetable Oils

	Mono Unsaturated Fat	Poly Unsaturated Fat	Saturated Fat
Olive Oil	77%	9%	14%
Groundnut Oil	49%	33%	18%
Corn Oil	25%	62%	13%
Soyabean Oil	24%	61%	15%
Sunflower Oil	29%	69%	11%
Safflower Oil	13%	77%	10%

41. Tea and Health

Tea is a widely used drink after water. Up to six cups daily is the best medicine. It is an agricultural produce, grown in warm humid climate with the rainfall precipitation level of 115-800 cc. per annum and acidic soil. The botanic name of tea is Camellia sinesis. The tea that is commonly consumed is Black Tea whereas other varieties of tea are Orthodox and Green Oolong. In India, tea is cultivated over a land area of 424469 hectares and Assam valley produces more than half of India's total tea production followed by Dooars. Around 3000 different varieties of tea are cultivated all over the world.

Now that you very well understand that tea is an agricultural, pure, herbal drink and the same has been professed by several scientific researches. The regular intake of 4 to 6 cups of tea per day is helpful in cancer, diabetes & heart disease etc. Scientific researchers are investigating how drinking of tea can protect us from certain diseases.

Black tea contains small amount of vitamins and minerals considered essential for maintaining good health. Popular all over the world, tea is made from leaf tips that have been withered, rolled and dried. Green tea, which is mainly drunk in China and Japan, is produced from fresh tips. Green tea is often held up by alternative practitioners as a healthier choice than "builder's brewup", largely because it has a lower level of caffeine. But studies over the past few years have shown that both black and green teas contain the same amount of antioxidants — compounds that help the body fight harmful molecules, called free radicals. These are strongly implicated in the development of certain chronic diseases, such as coronary heart disease, and some cancers, such as lung and gut tumours. Excess numbers of free radicals are caused by smoking, pollution and sun exposure, among other things.

The antioxidants found in tea are flavonoids, powerful compounds that scientists believe are instrumental in fighting disease. Some researchers believe that the antioxidant properties of tea are more powerful than those of fruits and vegetables. One cup of tea supplies about 200 mg of flavonoids. Drinking three cups each day increases the concentration of flavonoids in the blood by 25 per cent.

Both black and green teas are rich sources of potassium and manganese, as well as of vitamins, including Vitamin A, which has protective properties, Vitamin B_6, a crucial part of the body's metabolism, and Vitamins B_1 and B_2, which are essential for releasing energy from food. Potassium is vital for maintaining a normal heart-beat. Tea also contains phyto-chemicals, which the latest cancer research suggests might inhibit the growth of tumour cells. Advanced studies have also been done into its ability to fight heart disease. Research in America found that the risk of a heart attack in people who drank one or more cups of tea a day was half that of non-tea drinkers. Black tea has taken a bad rap in the past for being high in caffeine—according to one old wives' tale, it has more caffeine than coffee. But the truth is that a 200 ml cup of tea contains about 40 mg of caffeine, compared with 60 mg in the average cup of instant coffee, and 15 mg in filtered.

Nutritionists recommend a caffeine intake of no more than 300 mg a day, which allows for many cups of tea, although remember that you also consume it in chocolate, soft drinks, cold remedies and painkillers.

It contains:

Vitamins

- Beta-carotene, a precursor to vitamin A, has anti-oxidant and protective properties.
- Thiamin (vitamin B_1) and riboflavin (vitamin B_2) are both essential for releasing energy from food.
- Nicotinic acid and pantothenic acid are necessary for the release of energy from fat and carbohydrate.
- Ascorbic acid (vitamin C) is essential for a healthy immune system.
- Vitamin B_6 is involved in the metabolism of proteins.
- Folic acid plays a role in cell division.
- A daily average consumption of four cups of tea drunk with semi skimmed milk, provides:

  9% of the daily requirement of Vitamin B_1.

  25% of the daily requirement of Vitamin B_2.

  6% of the daily requirement of Vitamin B_6.

  10% of the daily requirement of Folic Acid.

Minerals

Tea is a rich source of two following minerals, essential for good health:

- ***Manganese*** – Manganese is essential for bone growth and the body's development and 2-5 mg a day is required for good health. Tea is one of the richest sources of manganese in our diet, with 5-6 cups of tea providing 45% of our daily requirement.
- ***Potassium*** – Potassium is vital for maintaining a normal heart beat. It enables nerves and muscles to function and regulates fluid levels within the cells. Its deficiency leads to erratic heart beat and fatigue. A normal, balanced diet should provide sufficient potassium for health. However, eating disorders such as anorexia and bulimia and over-exercise may lead to deficiency.

VEGETABLES

– Importance and Natural Benefits

Vegetables—Importance and Natural Benefits

Vegetables are important protective food and highly beneficial for the maintenance of health and prevention of disease. They contain valuable food ingredients which can be successfully utilized to build up and repair the body.

To derive maximum benefits of their nutrients, vegetables should be consumed fresh as far as possible. Most vegetables are best consumed in their natural raw state in the form of salads. An important consideration in making salads is that the vegetables should be fresh, crisp and completely dry. If vegetables have to be cooked, it should be ensured that their nutritive value is preserved to the maximum possible extent. The following hints will be useful in achieving this:

(i) Wash the vegetable thoroughly & cut into large pieces.

(ii) Boil water with salt and then add cut vegetables. (No water necessary for leafy vegetables)

(iii) Use minimum water just to cover vegetables.

(iv) Vegetables should not be exposed to sun after buying.

(v) Vegetables should not be exposed to atmospheric air. They should be covered while cooking.

(vi) They should be cooked for short time just to make them soft to touch for easy mastication.

(vii) They should be served hot.

To prevent loss of nutrients in vegetables, it is advisable to steam or boil vegetables in their own juices on slow fire and the water or cooking liquid should be drained off. In case it is boiled hard for long time in a large quantity of water, its nutritive and medicinal properties will be lost.

No vegetable should be peeled off, unless it is old and peeling is tough and unpalatable. In most root vegetables, the largest amount of vitamin and minerals are just below the skin and these are lost when deep peeling is done. Soaking of vegetables in water be avoided if taste and nutritive value are to be retained.

Finally, avoid using aluminium utensils for cooking as it being soft metal, is attacked by both acids and alkalis. There is scientific proof that small particles of aluminium from foods cooked in such pots enter the stomach and that the powerful astringent properties of aluminium injure the sensitive lining of stomach, leading to gastric irritation, digestive and intestinal diseases.

An intake of about 280 gms of vegetables each day per person is considered essential for the maintenance of good health. Of this, leafy vegetables (40%), root and tubers (30%) and other vegetables (30%) like brinjals, ladies' fingers etc. should be taken.

Medicinal Value – Vitamins & Minerals

Many vegetables contain a substance called carotene which is changed to vitamin A in the body. Vitamin A is necessary for normal growth and vitality, for good eyesight and healthy skin and for protection against diseases; especially of the respiratory tract. A deficiency of this vitamin causes eye infection, poor vision, night blindness, frequent colds, lack of appetite & skin disorders. Generally, coloured vegetables such as green leafy vegetables, carrot, papaya, tomatoes and yellow pumpkin are rich sources of carotene.

Several leafy vegetables like fenugreek leaves, turnip greens and beet greens contain riboflavin (Vitamin B_2), a member of vitamin B-Complex. This vitamin is essential for the growth and general health of eyes, skin, nails and hair. Its deficiency causes cracking of the corner of mouth and eczema.

Vitamin C (ascorbic acid) is present in good amount in many vegetables such as bitter gourd, tomatoes, cabbage and leafy vegetables like spinach, broccoli and drumstick leaves. Generally, fresh vegetables are better sources of vitamin C than dried, stale or withered ones. Vitamin C is essential for normal growth and maintenance of body tissues, especially of the joints, bones, teeth and gums and protection against infection. A deficiency of this vitamin causes scurvy, tooth decay, bleeding gums, anaemia and premature ageing.

Regarding minerals, the highly soluble one is calcium. Phosphorus, iron, magnesium, copper and potassium present in the vegetables maintain the acid-base balance of the hydrogen concentration of the body tissues. They are helpful in absorption of vitamins, proteins, fats and carbohydrates of the food. They are also helpful in throwing out excess liquid & salt from our body. The diuretic action of vegetables like potatoes, beans, spinach, radish, turnip and brinjal are specially important in cases of oedema or swellings, kidney and heart conditions.

Two important minerals, calcium and iron, found in vegetables, are very useful. Calcium is essential for strong bones and teeth. Iron is essential for blood formation. It is an essential constituent of haemoglobin, which helps to carry oxygen to the cells in various parts of body. Calcium and iron can be obtained in plenty from leafy vegetables like spinach and fenugreek leaves. Carrots, bitter gourds, onions and tomatoes are also fair sources of iron.

Curative Properties

Vegetables contain various medicinal and therapeutic agents. There are a large array of laxatives, sedatives and soporifics or sleep inducing components in the vegetable kingdom. Vegetables like onion, radish and celery exercise a tonic effect and are excellent for the nerves.

Certain vegetables are highly beneficial in the treatment of various diseases. Carrots are good for the blood. White crisp juicy stalks of celery serve as much better medicine in case of rheumatism or nervous dyspepsia than any nervine that relieves nerve disorders. A dish of spinach or dandelion will be beneficial in the treatment of kidney troubles. Lettuce can be used as a food remedy for insomnia. Onion can be used with advantage in the treatment of cough, cold, influenza, constipation, scurvy and hydrophobia. The leaves of fenugreek are highly valuable in the treatment of indigestion, flatulence and sluggish liver. Garlic can be beneficially used in heart diseases, hypertension, hypoglycemia, diabetes and even in fatal form of meningitis. It has been effectively used in lowering blood cholesterol and preventing blood clotting.

In gastro-intestinal disorders, vegetables play a vital role. Fibres in vegetables act as the mechanical intestinal expanders and draw more water and proteins in them and help easy expulsion of the waste in the form of stool. They prevent habitual constipation and keep the entire intestinal tract free from harmful germs. Fibres in the form of cellulose help the elimination of cholesterol. Such vegetables are: beetroot, cabbage, carrots, cucumbers, green peas and beans. They are also useful in case of arteriosclerosis, high BP and constipation. But when there is inflammation in the intestines, vegetables having less cellulose (fibre) content such as tomatoes, lettuce, potatoes and vegetable juices should be taken.

Pectin found in vegetables such as brinjal, radish pumpkin and beetroot absorb water, kill certain bacteria and toxins and eliminate them from the body. Garlic, onion, radish and mint contain pectin as well as anti-microbic qualities.

In blood disorders, vegetables also supply trace elements which are essential for human organism. Iodine, for instance, is essential for thyroid hormone which regulates much physical and mental activities, cobalt for increasing the number of blood corpuscles, and zinc for proper growth.

Asparagus (Shatawar)

Botanical Name : *Asparagus officinalis*
Family Name : Liliaceae
Hindi Name : Shatawar
Sanskrit Name : Sootmuli
English Name : Asparagus

Description

The generic name is derived from the Greek **spargao,** turgid. Asparagus grows on a perennial plant with a small rhizome, the stems can grow to over 6½ ft. (2m.). It has many long, delicate branches and subulate branchlets which resemble leaves. The shoots grow directly from the rhizome. The fruit is red berry containing four seeds.

Distribution

Normally a cultivated plant, asparagus is often found growing wild throughout Europe in sandy areas. Its medicinal part is gathered after the shoots have been cut. It is available abundantly in India, China, Britain, Taiwan, Africa and Malaysia.

Parts Used

Rhizome.

Properties

Diuretic, anti-plethoric, anti-dropsical, aphrodisiac, anti-leukaemic etc.

Forms of Use

Decoction, tincture, pulp, powder.

Food Value

Analysis of asparagus provides following composition (per 100 g):

Moisture 93%

Protein	2.2%
Fat	0.2%
Fibre	0.7%
Carbohydrate	4%
Calcium	22 mg
Phosphorus	62 mg
Magnesium	20 mg
Iron	1.0 mg
Vitamin A	900 I.U.
Vitamin C	33 mg
Vitamin B-complex	Some amount
Calorific Value	60

Medicinal Uses

It has multi-purpose therapeutic properties as described here:

(i) It has similar sedative effect on heart as the false heliebore (Adonis helieborus).

(ii) Asparagus is an excellent food for heart. A food medicine for weak and enlarged heart, its juice with honey three times daily will be highly useful.

(iii) The dried roots of asparagus are used in Unani medicine as an aphrodisiac which arouse sexual desire. It is sold in market as *Safed musli.* Roots boiled in milk are used as demulcent or soothing medicine. Its regular use thickens the semen and is valuable in impotency.

Note : Its consumption is not recommended for anyone suffering from kidney stones, cystitis, diabetes, nephritis or gout.

Beetroot (Chukandar)

Botanical Name : *Beta vulgaris*
Family Name : Chenopodi-aceae
Hindi Name : Chukandar
Sanskrit Name : Polanki
English Name : Beetroot

Description

Generally called as garden beet, it is a juicy root vegetable in two colours—deep red and violet. They are flat, short-top shaped, deep oblate to round, globular to oral, half long and long. Two varieties are grown in India — Crimzon Globe and dark red, both belong to the globular to oval group.

Distribution

Beetroot is a native of Europe, used by Greeks & Romans thousand years back. It is now cultivated all over the world. In India, it is cultivated for its nutritional roots.

Parts Used

Root & leaves.

Properties

Anti-anaemic, diuretic, tones liver, clears constipation and piles, cardiotonic.

Forms of Use

As vegetable, salad, juice, soup.

Food Value

This vegetable is good for health as it has carbohydrates in the form of sugar with little protein and fat. It is taken in form of salad, juice and as vegetable. Beetroot juice is considered as one of the best vegetable juices. It has natural sugar and calcium, sodium, potassium, phosphorus, sulphur, chlorine, iodine, iron, copper, vitamin B_1, B_2, niacin, B_6 and C.

Analysis of beetroot (100 gms edible part) gives the following composition (per 100 gms of edible part):

Moisture	87.8%
Protein	1.7%
Fat	0.1%
Mineral	0.8%
Fibre	1.0%
Carbohydrates	9.0%
Calcium	18 mg
Phosphorus	55 mg
Iron	1 mg
Vitamin C	10 mg
Calorific Value	43

Vitamin A and B-Complex also reported in good amount.

Medicinal Uses

No doubt, beetroot possesses great medicinal properties as it cleans kidney, gall bladder and is rich in alkaline elements, potassium, calcium, magnesium and iron. Its uses are:

(i) Beet juice is useful in anaemia as it forms blood owing to substantial iron. It triggers and activates the R.B.C., pushes fresh oxygen into the body and enhances lungs function for normal breathing. The juice of the red beet enhances body's power of resistance. It is good anti-anaemic for children and young people.

(ii) Beet juice is useful for jaundice, hepatitis, nausea and vomiting arising owing to acidity, diarrhoea, indigestion & dysentery. Adding a teaspoonful of lime juice to this juice increases its medicinal value and it can be given as a liquid food in these conditions. Fresh beet juice mixed with a tablespoonful of honey taken every morning before breakfast helps the healing of gastric ulcer. Juice of beet leaves mixed with lime juice is useful in jaundice and gastric ulcer to be taken once daily.

(iii) Eating beetroot is also useful for constipation and piles. If used daily, it prevents habitual constipation, thus helping in piles.

(iv) Beet juice corrects circulatory disorders as it is an excellent solvent for inorganic calcium deposits and thus helpful in the treatment of hypertension, arteriosclerosis & heart trouble.

(v) For kidney and gall bladder disorders, beet juice along with the juice of carrot and cucumber, acts as a cleansing material for both kidney & gall bladder.

Bengal Gram (Chana)

Botanical Name	: *Cicer arietinum*
Family Name	: Leguminosae
Hindi Name	: Chana
Sanskrit Name	: Chanaka
English Name	: Bengal Gram

Description

Bengal gram is most important among pulses available in the world. It is consumed in three forms — as vegetable sag, as pulse, as roasted gram and gram flour. Its seeds are beak-shaped and its plants are covered with tiny hairs.

Distribution

It originated in Asia, and spread to India & Europe in ancient times. It is cultivated in India, Pakistan, Egypt and other countries.

Parts Used

Seed & leaves.

Properties

Astringent, antidyspeptic, anti-constipation, antianaemic, anti-diabetic, antacid, tonic, aphrodisiac, hair promoter.

Form of Use

As vegetable and pulses.

Food Value

There are four uses of gram in the form of vegetable sag, pulses, roasted gram and gram flour which is used in many food preparations.

Analysis of Bengal gram provides the following composition:

Moisture	9.8%
Protein	17.1%
Fat	5.3%
Minerals	3.0%

Fibre	3.9%
Carbohydrate	60.9%
Calcium	202 mg
Phosphorus	312 mg
Iron	10.2 mg
Vitamin C	3 mg
Calorific Value	360
Vitamin B-Complex	Small Amount

Medicinal Uses

(i) Soaked in water every night and chewed in the morning with honey acts as a general tonic.

(ii) It is a boon for diabetics. Regular intake of gram in any form checks the fasting sugar levels and reduces insulin requirement by 20%.

(iii) Leaves of its plant provide enough iron. A tablespoon of fresh juice mixed with honey should be taken in anaemic conditions.

(iv) Roasted gram clears the excess oil from the intestines and acts as an antacid.

(v) It is an aphrodisiac and effective remedy in impotency and premature ejaculations. It is a general health tonic.

Bitter Gourd (Karela)

Botanical Name : *Momordica charantia*
Family Name : Cucurbi-taceae
Hindi Name : Karela
Sanskrit Name : Karavella
English Name : Bitter Gourd

Description

Its origin is not known but it is native to tropics. It is cultivated during hot season and is available in India, China, Sri Lanka, Malaysia etc.

Parts Used

Roots, leaves and fruits.

Properties

Hypoglycaemic (blood sugar reducer), astringent (arresting secretion), anti-haemorrhoidal (checks bleeding of piles), stomachic (appetiser and digestive), emmenagogue (inducing menstruation), galactogogue (increases milk secretion), hepatic stimulant (liver corrective), anthelmintic (removes worm) and blood purifier.

Forms of Use

Juice, as vegetable, soup & juice mixed with honey.

Food Value

Analysis of 100 gms edible portion of bitter gourd gives the following composition:

Moisture	92.4%
Protein	1.6%
Fat	0.2%
Minerals	0.8%
Fibre	0.8%

Carbohydrates	4.2%
Calcium	20 mg
Phosphorus	70 mg
Iron	1.8 mg
Vitamin C	88 mg
Calorific Value	25

Small amount of Vitamin B_1, B_2

Amino acids and a crystalline product named p-insulin

Medicinal Uses

(i) The bitter gourd has excellent medicinal properties and is used as a folk medicine for diabetes. It has hypoglycaemic or insulin-like principal, known as "plant-insulin". It reduces the blood and urine sugar levels. For better results, the diabetic should take the juice of about four or five fruits every morning on an empty stomach.

(ii) Diabetics usually suffer from malnutrition. They are normally under-nourished. Bitter gourd is rich in all the vitamins and minerals, especially vitamins A, B_1, B_2, C and iron. Its regular use prevents many complications such as hypertension, eye complications, neuritis and defective metabolism of carbohydrates. It increases body's resistance against infection.

(iii) Juice of the fresh leaves of bitter gourd is valuable in piles. Three teaspoonfuls of this juice mixed with a glassful of buttermilk should be taken each morning for about a month in this condition.

(iv) Bitter gourd is highly beneficial in the treatment of blood disorders like blood boils, scabies, itching psoriasis, ring-worm and other fungal diseases. A cupful of fresh juice of bitter gourd mixed with a teaspoonful of lime juice should be taken, sip by sip, on empty stomach daily for four to six months for these conditions.

(v) Its juice also works as preventive measure against leprosy cases.

(vi) Bitter gourd plant roots are used in folk medicine against respiratory troubles from ancient times. A teaspoonful of the root paste mixed with equal amount of honey or tulsi leaf juice, given once every night for a month acts as an excellent medicine for asthma, bronchitis, pharyngitis, colds and rhinitis.

(vii) Leaf juice is beneficial in the treatment of alcoholism. It is an antidose for intoxication caused by alcohol. It also tones up the liver affected by alcohol.

(viii) Diarrhoea and cholera can also be controlled by giving fresh leaf juice. Two teaspoonfuls of juice plus equal quantity of white onion juice along with one teaspoonful lemon juice should be given in these conditions.

Brinjal (Baigan)

Botanical Name : *Solamum melongena*
Family Name : Solanaceae
Hindi Name : Baigan
Sanskrit Name : Bhantaki
English Name : Brinjal

Description

Brinjal plant is erect and herbaceous plant with branched stems. It can grow to a height of 28 inches or more. The alternate, petiolate leaves are ovate-elliptic with an acute apex; they are entirely or lobate-dentate and slightly woolly haired. The flowers, which are carried on pedicels and arise from the leaf axils, have a many-lobed calyx and a many-lobed tubular, violet corolla. The fruit is a large, ellipsoid or globose berry containing firm, fleshy material and a great many brown seeds.

Distribution

Originally from India, this plant was introduced into Europe many years ago and now it is cultivated there. It is seldom found growing wild. It is gathered from summer to autumn.

Parts Used

Fruit, leaves.

Properties

Hypotensive, antihaemorrhoidal, cholesterol regulator, antidiabetic.

Forms of Use

Decoction, tincture, ointment.

Food Value

Moisture	87%
Protein	1.4%
Fat	0.3%
Fibre	1.3%

Carbohydrates	4.0%
Calcium	18 mg
Phosphorus	47 mg
Iron	1 mg
Carotene	74 mg
Vitamin B_1	0.04 mg
Vitamin B_2	0.11 mg
Niacin	0.9 mg
Vitamin C	12 mg
Calorific Value	24

Medicinal Uses

(i) The fruit is an excellent cholesterol regulator.

(ii) It is very effective too, when used externally in a fat or oil-based preparation to relieve haemorrhoidal discomfort.

(iii) It is very nutritious and is sometimes referred to as poor man's meat.

(iv) It is anti-diabetic and used to check diabetes.

(v) It reduces swellings of legs, its decoction is applied gradually over the parts.

(vi) Crush the fruit and squeeze juice. Apply juice on the palm and sole. It will check perspiration acting as sweat preventive.

Cabbage (Pattagobhi)

Botanical Name : *Brassica oleracea*
Family Name : Cruciferae
Hindi Name : Pattagobhi
Sanskrit Name : Dalamalini
English Name : Cabbage

Description

Cabbage is among the important vegetables. It is grown almost all over the world. It is an excellent muscle builder and cleanser. It differs in shape, size and colour depending on the climate the area where it is grown.

Distribution

Its cultivation is known from ancient times and it originated in Europe. It was regarded as an important vegetable by Greeks and Romans. The major areas of cultivation are northern India, Indonesia, Malaysia, South America, Africa & Philippines.

Parts Used

Leaves.

Properties

Bitter, stomachic, cardiotonic, antigout, anti-rheumatic, diuretic, laxative, anthelmintic.

Forms of Use

As salad, as vegetable and in the form of juice.

Food Value

Cabbage is valued for its mineral, vitamins content and alkaline nature. It is also used as salad and eating it raw is much more beneficial than cooking in which useful nutrients are almost minimised or lost. The raw cabbage is also easily digestible than the cooked one (longer it is cooked, less digestible it becomes).

Analysis of cabbage gives the following composition:

Moisture	91.9%
Protein	1.8%
Fat	0.1%
Minerals	0.6%
Fibre	1.0%
Carbohydrate	4.6%
Calcium	40 mg
Phosphorus	45 mg
Iron	0.8 mg
Vitamin C	125 mg
Calorific Value	27

Small amount of B-complex

Medicinal Uses

(i) It possesses valuable property of having sulphur, chlorine and iodine contents. The combination of sulphur and chlorine causes a cleaning of the mucus membranes of the stomach and the intestinal tract. But this only applies when cabbage or its juice is taken in raw and that too without salt.

(ii) Avoid excess intake of cabbage or its juice. Normal use is recommend as its excessive consumption may cause thyroid disease called goitre.

(iii) Normal amount of cabbage or its juice naturally treats infections, ulcers and other disorders of the digestive system.

(iv) Cabbage clears constipation as it is full of roughage i.e. indigestible material which is necessary to activate intestine for proper action of the bowels. A meal of raw cabbage is a remedy for obstinate constipation.

(v) In stomach ulcers/duodenal ulcers, drink cabbage juice for miraculous results. Raw cabbage juice was accepted as ulcer healer some three decades back as it contains the anti-ulcer factor, vitamin U. **This vitamin is destroyed**

by cooking. Doses are 80 to 180 gm juice three times daily after meals/breakfast. To make cabbage juice more palatable other juices of tomato/pinepapple/citrus juice may be added. If one does not have a juicer or blender, one can eat it like salad 4/5 times daily.

(vi) It is also used in skin disorders. Cabbage leaves are used in the form of compresses in healing ulcers, infected sores, blisters and skin eruptions, including psoriasis. They are also valuable in burns and carbuncles.

(vii) It arrests premature ageing. Research has shown that cabbage contains several elements and factors which increase the immunity of the human body and prevent rapid ageing. It also contains vitamins P and C which give strength to the blood vessels and keep infections at bay.

(viii) Cabbage is good for elderly persons as it clears constipation, checks piles and obesity (calorific value is only 27 kilocalories).

(ix) Prepare a paste of leaves. Place it over the site of swelling to get relief from gout.

(x) Leaf juice or vegetable prepared from it, if taken regularly, is proved to be cancer preventive. The sulphur and amino acid histidine present in the leaf, check the growth of tumours and keep body cells normal.

Carrot (Gajar)

Botanical Name : *Daucus carota*
Family Name : Umbelliferae
Hindi Name : Gajar
Sanskrit Name : Shikha-mula
English Name : Carrot

Description

A large number of carrot varieties, some indigenous but mostly imported from Europe and America, are cultivated in India. The colour of the roots in the cultivated types varies from yellowish, orange, light purple, deep purple, to deep red etc.

An annual or biennial herb, with twice or thrice pinnate leaves and flattish umbebs of small, white flowers, each with a single, central crimson or red brown floret. The fruit is oblong, dorsally flattered, with prickles tipped by minute bristles.

Distribution

Indigenous to Kashmir and western Himalayas, carrot is now largely cultivated in India for culinary purposes.

Parts Used

Root and seeds.

Properties

Aromatic, stimulant, carminative, lithontriptic, antifertile, abortifacient, diuretic, galactagogic, ophthalmic and source of minerals.

Forms of Use

Juice, decoction, essence, tincture.

Food Value

Carrot is valued as food mainly because it is a rich source of the fat soluble hydrocarbon, $C_{40} H_{56}$, the beta form of which is the precursor of Vitamin A. Analysis of the edible portion of carrot gave the following composition (per 100 gms of edible part):

Moisture	86.0%
Protein	0.9%
Fat	0.1%
Carbohydrate	10.7%
Fibre	1.2%
Mineral matter	1.1%
Calcium	80 mg
Phosphorus	530 mg
Iron	2.2 mg
Nicotinic acid	5 mg
Vitamin C	3 mg

Also contains beta-carotene in good amount and Vitamin B-complex.

The protein content of carrot tends to decrease and the total carbohydrate content tends to increase with growth. Sucrose, glucose and starch are present. Vitamin C is present in the form of a protein-ascorbic acid complex. Vitamin D, a substance with the characteristics of vitamin E and a phospholipid of vitamin reactions corresponding to A and D containing calcium, phosphorus and nitrogen in organic linkage are also present.

Cooking brings about a considerable loss in the nutrient value of carrots. There is a loss in total solids, total nitrogen, sugars and ash constituents. Ascorbic acid is partially oxidised and a part of vitamin D is also lost. So, steam cooking is better.

Products/Preservation

Carrot products like carrot juice, carotene concentrates, carrot oil etc. are prepared by canning and dehydration.

Both canning and dehydration have been used for preserving carrots. The carotene content of canned carrot is slightly affected by storage for six month, Vitamin B_1 & B_2 are better retained but there is loss of vitamin C. It is stored in cans after pressure-cooking and oven-cooking.

For dehydration, carrots are subjected to steam blanching for 5-7 minutes. The sliced material is dipped in a solution of sulphur dioxide before blanching, as this treatment improves colour retention in dehydrated products. Carrots are dried to

5% moisture or less and packed in containers with nitrogen. The dehydrated product retains most of the vitamins.

Carrot juice is prepared by pressing carrots. After routine treatment, juice is stored and remains fresh for over a year. It retains all the vitamins and minerals.

Beta-carotene concentrates are prepared from fresh or dried carrots. The juice-free carrots are macerated and digested with alkali under pressure and the carotene is extracted with mineral oil.

Medicinal Uses

(i) Carrot has a beneficial influence on kidneys and dropsy, and prevents the brick-dust sediment sometimes found in the urine.

(ii) Carrots clear the blood and are recommended in chronic diarrhoea.

(iii) A decoction of carrot is useful in jaundice.

(iv) Seeds are used as aphrodisiac and nervine tonic.

(v) Intake of seeds is avoided during pregnancy as it can cause abortion.

(vi) It is a good source of vitamin A. Beta-carotene present in carrots is a precursor of vitamin A. One unit of beta-carotene gives two units of vitamin A, and is good for eyesight. This conversion is done by the liver and it is stored in our body.

(vii) An infusion of carrot has long been used as a folk remedy for thread worms.

(viii) Carrot leaves contain a vitamin E-rich oil and, in some areas, are used in the making of soup.

(ix) Carrot is rich in alkaline elements which purify and revitalise the blood. It nourishes the entire system and helps in the maintenance of acid-alkaline balance in the body.

(x) Carrot contains good amount of anti-cancer nutrient, beta-carotene. One should make use of it daily in each meal.

(xi) The juice of carrot is known as a "Miracle juice." It makes a fine health-giving drink for children and adults alike. It strengthens the eyes and keeps the mucus membranes of all cavities of the body in healthy condition. It is beneficial in the treatment of dry and rough skin.

(xii) Chewing a carrot immediately after food kills all the harmful germs in the mouth. It cleans the teeth, removes the food particles from cavities and checks bleeding of the gums and tooth decay.

(xiii) Regular use of carrot prevents formation of gastric ulcer and other digestive disorders.

(xiv) Carrot juice is an effective remedy in diseases like intestinal colic, colitis, appendicitis, peptic ulcer and dyspepsia.

(xv) Carrot soup is an effective natural remedy for diarrhoea as it gives sodium, potassium, phosphorus, calcium, sulphur and magnesium essential to check diarrhoea. Besides, it is good source of pectin and coats the intestine to allay inflammation. It checks growth of harmful bacteria and prevents vomiting. It is specially useful for children (½ kg carrot to be cooked in 150 ml water until it becomes soft, water is drained, little salt is added, ½ cup soup is given every half an hour).

(xvi) Carrots are useful in the removal of worms from children. A small cup of juice or two medium-sized carrots taken in the morning for at least a week clears the thread worms.

China Spinach (Chaulai)

Botanical Name	: *Amaranthus gangeticus*
Family Name	: Amaranthaceae
Hindi Name	: Chaulai saag
Sanskrit Name	: Tanduliyah
English Name	: China spinach

Description

Amaranth is a popular green leafy vegetable, grown all over India. It is usually a short-lived annual herb, with erect and often thick and fleshy stems and green leaves. There are about six species of amaranth in cultivation.

Distribution

Most species of amaranth are believed to have originated in the regions of South America or Mexico. The various species are now widely distributed throughout most tropical areas—India, China, Malaysia, Taiwan, Africa etc. Amaranth is a warm season crop and its all species can be grown in the summer and mostly in the rainy season.

Parts Used

Leaves, root & seeds.

Properties

Carminative, nutritive, antibiotic, emollient, demulcent, anti-rheumatic and aphrodisiac.

Forms of Use

As vegetable, decoction, poultice, juice mixed with lemon & honey.

Food Value

Analysis of 100 gms edible portion of amaranth gives the following composition:

Moisture	85.7%
Protein	4.0%
Fat	0.5%
Minerals	2.7%
Fibre	1.0%
Carbohydrate	6.1%
Calcium	397 mg
Phosphorus	83 mg
Iron	25.5 mg
Vitamin C	173 mg
Vitamin A	2500-11000 I.U.
Calorific Value	45

Small amount of Vitamin B-complex

Medicinal Uses

(i) Regular use of amaranth in our food items prevents the deficiency of Vitamins A, B_1, B_2 and C, calcium, iron and potassium.

(ii) It protects against several disorders, such as defective vision, recurrent colds and functional sterility.

(iii) Extract its juice and mix with honey. The decoction is a wonderful remedy against bronchitis, asthma, emphysema and tuberculosis.

(iv) A teaspoon of fresh amaranth juice with honey given to infants makes them healthy and strong. This also prevents constipation and eases the teething process, thus preventing retarded growth.

(v) The juice of the plant mixed with a teaspoon of lemon juice is effective against bleeding caused by weak gums, nose, lungs and even piles.

(vi) A decoction of the leaves or roots is given in ½ ounce in diarrhoea, leucorrhoea, menorrhoagia and impotence. A poultice of the leaves with honey is applied over inflammed and painful parts.

(vii) The seeds are cooling, demulcent and powerful aphrodisiac; they are given in leucorrhoea and impotence.

(viii) The leaves are sweetish, expectorant, vulnerary, antipyretic, emmenagogue, emetic, stop suppuration, useful in biliousness, flashy tumours, toothache, burning sensations, liver complaints, inflammations, decoction as gargle in stomatitis.

(ix) Amaranth is valuable in respiratory disorders. Drinking fresh juice along with honey is a remedy for chronic bronchitis & asthma.

(x) Regular use of amaranth during pregnancy and lactation is highly beneficial. One cup of fresh leaf juice of amaranth mixed with honey and a pinch of cardamom powder should be taken during entire period of pregnancy. It will help in the normal growth of the baby, prevent the loss of calcium and iron from the body, relax the uterine ligaments and facilitate easy delivery without much pain. Its use after childbirth will shorten the laying-in period, check the postnatal complications and increase the flow of breast milk.

(xi) Growing children can safely be given this juice as a natural protein tonic. It contains all the essential amino acids, such as orginine, histidine, isolencine, lencine, lysine, cystine, methionine, phenylalamine, threonine, tryptophan and valine.

(xii) Regular use of amaranth prevents premature old age as it checks the imbalance of calcium and iron metabolism that often occurs in old age. According to Dr. Van-Sylke, calcium molecules begin to deposit in bone tissues as one becomes old. This hampers calcium distribution influenced by the improper molecular movements of iron in the tissues. This molecular disturbance of calcium and iron is prevented by regular supply of food calcium and iron as they are found in amaranth.

(xiii) Amaranth is useful in all kinds of bleeding tendencies. A cup of leaf juice mixed with a teaspoonful of lime juice should be taken every night in conditions like bleeding from the gums, nose, lungs, piles and excessive menstruation.

(xiv) It is also useful in the treatment of leucorrhoea. The sind of the root of amaranth rubbed in 250 ml of water and strained should be given to the patient daily in the morning and evening for 2/3 days or as needed.

Cucumber (Khira)

Botanical Name : *Cucumis sativus*
Family Name : Cucurbitaceae
Hindi Name : Khira
Sanskrit Name : Sukasa
English Name : Cucumber

Description

It is a very popular vegetable cultivated in large scale. It has refreshing and cooling effect. It contains all minerals and trace elements essential for health.

Many varieties of cucumber are known—from light to dark green colour. It turns yellow when mature. Its size varies from 8 to 30 cm.

Distribution

Originated in India, cucumber was known to Egypt, Greece, Rome and China in ancient time. It is widely distributed all over the world. It is cultivated in India, Pakistan, China, America & other countries.

Parts Used

Fruit.

Properties

Diuretic, laxative, electrolyte, cooling, nutritive, demulcent, tonic, refreshing, aromatic.

Forms of Use

As vegetable, salad, juice.

Food Value

The cucumber has a relatively high mineral ratio. Its skin is most valuable as the cell salts and vitamins are just beneath it. So, peeling is to be avoided while eating.

A valuable source of potassium, sodium, magnesium, sulphur, silicon, chlorine and fluorine. Nutritional value of food is enhanced with the addition of cucumber as salad (better prepared with the addition of carrot, tomato, radish, cabbage and curd).

Analysis of cucumber gives the following compositions (per 100 gms of edible part):

Moisture	96.3%
Protein	0.4%
Fat	0.1%
Mineral	0.3%
Fibre	0.4%
Carbohydrate	2.5%
Calcium	10 mg
Phosphorus	25 mg
Iron	1.5 mg
Vitamin C	7 mg
Calorific Value	13

Some amount of vitamin B-Complex.

Medicinal Uses

Cucumber has 65% alkaline and 35% acid forming minerals. This mineral balance makes cucumber a medicinally useful vegetable. It maintains alkalinity of the blood. It is a natural powerful diuretic, promoting flow of urine. It should be taken raw (skin intact) to get more benefits.

Other benefits are:

(i) Being laxative in nature, it corrects constipation. Two cucumbers per day are advised for removing habitual constipation.

(ii) For stomach disorders, its juice is useful as it corrects acidity, gastrid and duodenal ulcers. A cup of fresh juice 3/4 times daily is helpful. It gives immediate relief in burning sensation of stomach.

(iii) In rheumatic problems, its juice along with the juices of carrot & beet, brings relief as it washes out uric acid deposition in arthritis, gout etc.

(iv) In urinary disorders, cucumber is very beneficial. It increases flow of urine and is useful in dissolving the gravel in urinary tract and reducing the urine acidity.

(v) For nausea/cholera it is a boon, as it immediately stops nausea & vomiting, which allopathic medicine fails to control. A glassful fresh juice mixed with coconut water given one cup hourly, controls cholera. It is a wonderful remedy for electrolyte imbalance in case of dehydration.

Drumstick (Sahijan)

Botanical Name : *Moringa oleifera*
Family Name : Moringaceae
Hindi Name : Sahijan
Sanskrit Name : Sobhanjana
English Name : Drumstick

Description

It's a common vegetable. Its tender pod is used. It is anti-bacterial and a good cleanser. Drumstick tree is perennial, erect, slender, medium-sized with many arching branches. It has drumstick-like fruits, small white flowers and small and round leaves which are cooked and eaten as vegetable.

Distribution

All over India and Pakistan.

Parts Used

Leaves, root, root bark, bark, fruit, flowers, gum, seed oil & seed.

Properties

Stimulant, anti-epileptic rubrifacient, carminative, stomachic, abortif, cardiotonic, antispasmodic, anti-flatulent and antiparalytic.

Forms of Use

As vegetable, as poultice, as powder.

Food Value

Drumstick pods and leaves are sources of carotene, calcium, phosphorus, ascorbic acid. All parts of its plant are widely used in some form or the other.

Drumstick analysis gives the following composition (per 100 gms.):

	Drumstick (Pods)	Leaves
Moisture	87%	76%
Protein	2.5%	7.0%
Fat	0.1%	2.0%
Minerals	2.0%	2.0%
Fibre	5%	1%
Carbohydrate	4%	13%
Calcium	30 mg	450 mg
Phosphorus	100 mg	70 mg
Iron	5 mg	7 mg
Vitamin C	125 mg	225 mg
Calorific Value	26	92
Vitamin B-Complex	Small amount	Small amount

Medicinal Uses

(i) The juice of leaves mixed with milk works as a wonderful tonic for infants and children (two tablespoons juice in a half cup milk will suffice). This tonic gives better results in pregnancy and lactation as it contains iron and minerals.

(ii) The soup of drumstick leaves is very useful in respiratory disorders like asthma, bronchitis and T.B. This soup is prepared by adding a handful of leaves in a cup of water and is boiled for 10 minutes. It is filtered and cooled. It is taken with little salt, pepper and lime juice (2/3 times/day).

(iii) The soup of drumstick leaves, flowers & fruits has antibacterial properties like antibiotics and thus successful in preventing infections of throat, chest & skin.

(iv) Flowers boiled in milk are good for sexual debility. It also corrects functional sterility in men and women. For impotency, premature ejaculation and thinness of semen, 100 g dry bark powder boiled in 500 ml water for 30 to 40 minutes and 25 ml of this plus two tablespoons honey should be taken 3 times daily for a month.

(v) A tablespoon of fresh juice of leaves plus honey (2 tablespoonfuls) and a half glass of coconut water is good to combat cholera, dysentery, diarrhoea, colitis & jaundice.

(vi) A tablespoon of fresh juice of leaves plus juice of carrot (half glass) or cucumber (half glass) is an effective remedy for scanty urination and constant burning in urethra.

(vii) A poultice of the fresh leaves is applied to wounds, boils and swellings.

(viii) The leaves are applied hot to the scrotum in hydrocele overnight.

(ix) The bland fixed oil extracted from the seed is popularly known as BEN-OIL. It is an aperient. It is applied locally to painful gouty and rheumatic joints.

(x) The gum that exudes from stem is taken with milk for headache, as well as applied locally.

Fenugreek (Methi)

Botanical Name : *Trigonella foenum-graecum*
Family Name : Leguminosae
Hindi Name : Methi
Sanskrit Name : Methika
English Name : Fenugreek

Description

Fenugreek plant is erect, strongly scented, robust, 1-2 ft. high plant. It grows annually. Leaves compound; 3/4-1 inch long; stipules entire, leaflets 3, lanceolate, or oborate, toothed. Flowers axillary, 1-2 sessile, yellow. Pods 2-3 inches long, thin pointed, 10-20 seeded, seeds emitting a peculiar odour, brownish yellow, having an oblique furrow along a part of their length.

Distribution

Native of Europe and Ethiopia, fenugreek is also found growing wild in north-western India. It is being used as medicine and food from ancient times. Fenugreek is a cool season crop & it grows all over India and Pakistan.

Parts Used

Seeds, leaves.

Properties

Cooling, carminative, tonic, aphrodisiac, anti-dysenteric, aromatic, diuretic, nutritive, emollient, astringent, aperient and lactagogue.

Form of Use

As vegetable, juice, poultice.

Food Value

It is used as methi saag and its seeds are used as a condiment and for flavour. Its leaf contains maximum number of amino acids, constituents of protein.

Fenugreek analysis provides following composition:

Moisture	86%
Protein	4.4%
Fat	1%
Minerals	1.5%
Fibre	1%
Carbohydrate	6%
Calcium	400 mg
Phosphorus	50 mg
Iron	17 mg
Vitamin C	50 mg
Vitamin B-Complex	Small amount
Calorific Value	50

Medicinal Uses

(i) Leaves are aromatic, cooling and aperient.

(ii) Leaves' paste applied on hair before bath enhances their lustre, life and length.

(iii) Leaves are highly useful in indigestion, flatulence and in liver disorders.

(iv) Leaves contain enough iron that helps in forming blood, especially useful in anaemia.

(v) Leaves and seeds are lactagogue which increases the flow of milk.

(vi) The seeds help restore a deadened sense of taste or smell. The loss of sense of taste occurs due to improper functioning of the salivary glands.

(vii) Tea prepared from seeds reduces fever. It also works in malarial fever.

(viii) Tea prepared from the seeds is also useful in stomach, intestine & allied ailments viz. inflammation, bowels, kidneys, peptic ulcer (where it forms protective coating against ulcers).

(ix) It is good for respiratory tract infections viz. bronchitis, influenza, sinusitis, catarrh, pneumonia. Tea of seeds will help in these cases (four cups daily).

(x) Its seeds are effective in controlling diabetes (25 to 100 grams daily).

Garlic (Lahsun)

Botanical Name : *Allium sativum*

Family Name : Liliaceae

Hindi Name : Lahsun

Sanskrit Name : Lashuna

English Name : Garlic

Description

A garden vegetable, cultivated from time immemorial. It is a food, a herb, a medicinal plant, an antiseptic etc. It is very well-known, bulbous, herbaceous plant which grows to about 40 inches (1m) high. The bulb consists of 8-10 curved bulbets (cloves). The stem is erect and hollow.

Distribution

Originated in Central Asia, garlic has been cultivated in Mediterranean countries for many centuries and in Britain since the beginning of the 16th Century. It was known to Chinese much earlier (3000 BC). Even today, it is a regular item of Chinese diet and is regarded as a medicine for several ailments. It is now widely grown in India, China, Philippines, Brazil & Mexico. It is gathered in July-August.

Parts Used

Bulb.

Properties

Antibiotic, hypoglycaemic, hypotensive, anthelmintic, carminative, intestinal disinfectant, anti-rheumatic, corn-remover, anti-malarial, rubefacient.

Form of Use

Tincture, fluid and semi-fluid extract, ointment, poultice.

Food Value

Hippocrates, the father of modern medicine (460-357 BC), who taught and practised in ancient Athens, recommended the use of this vegetable in infectious diseases, especially intestinal diseases.

An analysis of 100 gms garlic shows the presence of:

Moisture	62.0%
Protein	6.3%
Fat	0.1%
Minerals	1.0%
Fibre	0.8%
Carbohydrates	30%
Calcium	30 mg
Phosphorus	310 mg
Iron	1.5 mg
Vitamin C	15 mg
Calorific Value	145

Traces of iodine, sulphur, chlorine and selenium apart from small amounts of vitamin B-Complex.

Medicinal Uses

Garlic is recommended for asthma, bronchial congestion, arteriosclerosis, worms, liver and gall bladder problems. Garlic is also good for heart, digestion, skin diseases, piles and cough.

Charak, ancient Indian old physician, once told that only anomaly in garlic is its bad smell

According to Dr. M.W. McDuffic of the Metropolitan Hospital, New York, "Garlic contains a volatile oil, called allyl sulphide and its medical properties depend on this oil. Strongly antiseptic, it seems to have a remarkable power of inhibiting the growth of the Koch's bacillus, eliminated by the lungs, skin, kidneys and liver, and oxidises sulphonic acid in the system."

Garlic is a rejuvenator, easily absorbed by our skin and reaches deep in the tissues—bones, glands, lungs; removes toxins, revitalizes the blood, stimulates blood circulation and normalises intestinal flora.

Its other uses are:

(i) Garlic is prescribed for chest disease e.g. TB and pneumonia (One gram garlic, 250 ml milk and 1000 ml water boiled till volume reduced to one-fourth, it is to be taken 3 times a day).

(ii) Garlic is a good remedy for asthma (3 cloves boiled in milk to be taken every night).

(iii) Garlic is regarded as a powerful intestinal antiseptic. It cures infectious diseases and inflammations of stomach and intestine. It is also useful in expelling worms, colitis, dysentery and soothes intestinal flora.

(iv) Garlic lowers blood pressure (by dilating the arteries), soothes spasm of small arteries, slows the pulse rate and normalises heart rhythm. Besides, it relieves the dizziness, shortness of breath and stomach gas (3 garlic capsules per day recommended in these cases).

(v) Garlic is used widely against rheumatism and allied diseases (3 garlic capsules are taken per day and paste of garlic is rubbed on the affected part).

(vi) Garlic may prevent heart attacks. It lowers cholesterol level of blood vessels thereby preventing hardening of arteries leading to high blood pressure and heart attack.

(vii) Garlic is proved to be a patent anti-carcinogenic agent. It retards tumour growth not only in experimented mice but also in human beings (regular use of garlic is advised in such cases).

(viii) Garlic is also recommended for various skin diseases. It helps clear the skin spots, pimples, eczema etc. It should be taken orally also to clear the disease.

(ix) Garlic is considered an effective remedy for diptheria. Chewing a clove of garlic removes membrane, reduces temperature and relieves the patient (30 to 60 gms of garlic can be used in this way in three or four hours a week).

(x) Garlic is a potent aphrodisiac. It is a tonic for loss of sexual power and nervous exhaustion—especially for old people.

Ginger (Adrak)

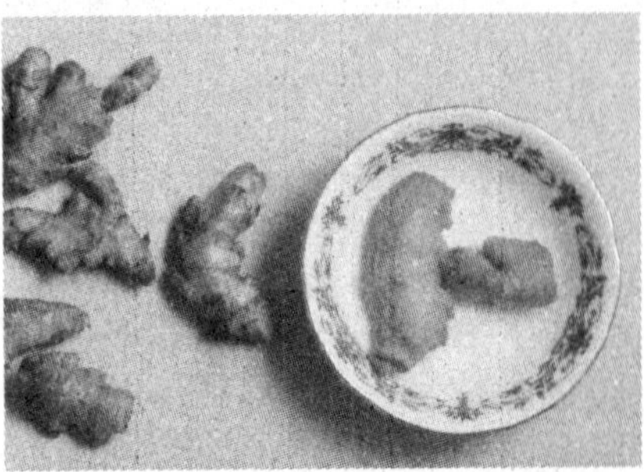

Botanical Name : *Zingiber officinale*

Family Name : Zingiberaceae

Hindi Name : Adrak

Sanskrit Name : Adraka

English Name : Ginger

Description

Ginger is a perennial herb having underground branch—stems known as rhizomes—a swollen hard part. They are brownish-yellow in colour from inside and rough brown outside with diameter 2.5 cm. Leaves & rhizome possess specific odour, sold as adrak in fresh form and as *sonth* in dry form.

Distribution

It has its origin in India and at the same time in China where it has been in use as spice from ancient times. The major producers are India & China. It is cultivated all over India, Pakistan, China, Taiwan etc.

Parts Used

Root.

Properties

Stimulant, carminative, anti-dyspeptic, anti-flatulent, rubefacient, digestant, aphrodisiac, anti-rheumatic.

Food Value

Ginger is available in two forms, fresh and dried. Both the forms contain effective food value. As the taste of ginger is not very palatable, subtle means are adopted to use it in certain ways. It has dual role, as a vegetable as well as a spice. It is held in high esteem for its flavour, pungency, aroma and medicinal value.

Ginger analysis gives the following composition:

Moisture	81%
Protein	2.3%
Fat	1.0%
Minerals	1.2%
Fibre	2.5%
Carbohydrates	12.3%
Calcium	20 mg
Phosphorus	60 mg
Iron	2.6 mg
Vitamin C	6.0 mg
Calorific Value	67

Small amount of Vitamin B-Complex

Medicinal Uses

(i) Ginger has been medicinally used from Vedic period and is considered as a carminative and antifermenting medicine. Greek physicians used it against gout, paralysis and as aphrodisiac. In India, it is widely used in the form of spices, as rubrefacient, aphrodisiac, digestant and in cold and cough.

(ii) It is extremely useful in disorders of the digestive system, e.g. dyspepsia, flatulence, colic, vomiting, spasms etc. Chewing a piece of fresh ginger after meals regularly is good for these troubles.

(iii) Ginger is an effective remedy for colds and coughs. Juice of ginger and honey (one teaspoonful each) four times daily helps combat cough. For colds, it should be cut into pieces and boiled with a cup of water. The strained liquid should be taken 3/4 times a day. Ginger tea prepared by adding lemon grass (2 leaves), tulsi (5 leaves) is very good for both.

(iv) Ginger juice along with fenugreek boiled for some time, filtered, honey added to taste provides good diaphoratic mixture for fever & influenza. It acts as an expectorant in bronchitis, asthma, whooping cough etc.

(v) Ginger is also a painkiller. Rubbing ginger with water and applying it on the forehead gives relief in headache. It is useful in toothache and ear-ache (a drop is sufficient for ear-ache).

(vi) Ginger is a potent aphrodisiac (half a teaspoon ginger juice is to be taken with a half-boiled egg and honey, once, daily at night for a month). It tones up sex centres.

(vii) Ginger is also useful in menstrual disorders. Pieces of ginger be boiled in a cup of water and taken 3/4 times after filtration & adding sugar. If taken early in the morning, it is an effective remedy for morning sickness, biliousness, sluggish liver, jaundice, indigestion, excessive formation of gas in the intestines, constipation, diarrhoea due to indigestion, burning in the gastro-intestinal tract and constant burning sensation in the chest.

Groundnut/Peanut (Moongphali)

Botanical Name : *Arachis hypogaea*
Family Name : Leguminosae
Hindi Name : Peanut (Moongphali)
Sanskrit Name : Buchanaka
English Name : Groundnut

Description

Groundnut is a legume that belongs to pea and bean family. It is the only nut that grows underground. It is an annual herb growing 50 cm high that develops a stalk which enters the soil and forms pod with seeds. It takes two months' time for maturity. When the plant's leaves turn yellow, it is taken out for drying & peanuts get removed from it.

Distribution

It is a common belief that peanut originated in Africa but evidence suggests that South America is its first home. Now, it is cultivated all over the world. India leads the world in groundnut production (40% production is from India).

Parts Used

Seed.

Properties

Tonic, aphrodisiac, anti-anaemic, tones brain nerves, anti-cancerous, cholesterol reducer.

Forms of Use

Oil, eating raw.

Food Value

It is nutritionally very important containing more protein than meat. The proteins of groundnut are well balanced and have nearly all essential amino-acids. It is also a source of magnesium, phosphorus and copper.

For proper digestion, groundnut requires proper mastication *i.e.* to make a paste. Otherwise it will not digest properly.

Groundnut (100 gms) analysis provides the following composition:

Moisture	3%
Protein	25.3%
Fat	40.1%
Minerals	2.4%
Fibre	3.1%
Carbohydrate	26.1%
Calcium	90 mg
Phosphorus	350 mg
Iron	2.8 mg
Vitamin E	261.4 mg
Calorific Value	567
Vitamin B-Complex	Small Amount

Medicinal Uses

(i) All peanuts are cholesterol free which is good for heart.

(ii) It is a good source of dietary fibre and prevents some types of cancer.

(iii) Folic acid is present in it. It may prevent 50% to 80% of some nervous system, birth defects.

(iv) The groundnut oil is an excellent aperient or a mild laxative and emollient which softens skin.

(v) Taking with jaggery, it is very nutritive for children and women. It builds resistance against all infections, especially TB and liver trouble.

(vi) It is good for diabetics. Eating handful of groundnuts daily will be beneficial.

Onion (Pyaz)

Botanical Name : *Alluim cepa*
Family Name : Liliaceae
Hindi Name : Pyaz
Sanskrit Name : Palandu
English Name : Onion

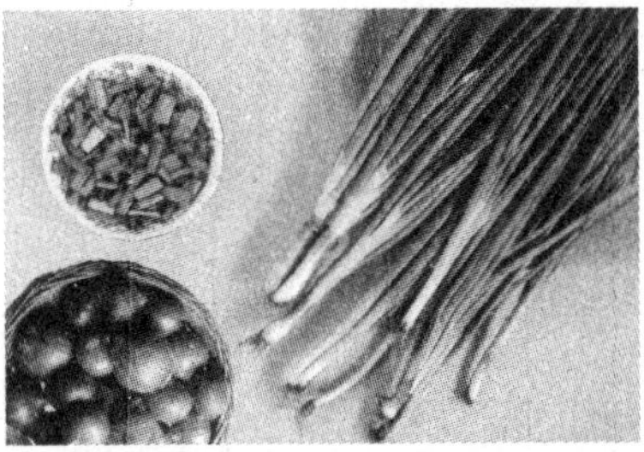

Description

The bulbous root of this plant consists of layers of fleshy scales covered by white, yellow or violet-coloured tunics. The erect stem is hollow with a swelling at the lower end and can grow as high as 40 inches (1 m). The hollow leaves, which are almost cylindrical or slightly flattened, have a glabrous surface. The flowers, which have white or purple tepals, are clustered into rounded heads. The fruit consists of one capsule and 3 loculi with flat, black seeds.

Distribution

Onion was originated in Persia. Once it was a popular food of Egypt (depicted on tombs in 1500 BC). A city was named Onion by Jews that existed for 343 years. It is frequently grown, both privately and commercially, in gardens throughout Europe, Egypt, America, India, China, Japan, Malaysia etc. for the edible root (onions). It is gathered from mid-summer onwards depending on the time of planting.

Parts Used

Bulb and twigs.

Properties

Stimulant, diuretic, expectorant, aphrodisiac, emmenagogue, anti-flatulent, antidysenteric, cardiotonic, bactericidal, reduces blood sugar, lowers cholesterol, anti-inflammatory, hypotensive, anthelmintic, anti-sclerotic, analgesic, anti-neuralgic, anti-rheumatic, corn remover.

Food Value

Onion derives its name from French word 'oignon' meaning most explosive natural food *i.e.* it has very good food value in comparison to other vegetables.

Onion analysis gives the following composition:

Moisture	86.6%
Protein	1.2%
Fat	0.1%
Fibre	0.6%
Minerals	0.4%
Carbohydrates	11%
Calcium	48 mg
Phosphorus	50 mg
Iron	0.7 mg
Vitamin C	11 mg
Small amount of Vitamin B-Complex	
Calorific Value	51

Medicinal Uses

(i) Onion possesses expectorant properties. It dissolves phlegm and prevents its formation. It is valued as food remedy medicine for the time immemorial for cold, cough, bronchitis and influenza. A juice mixture of onion, honey and *adrak* in the ratio 2:2:1 keeps one free from cold and cough (one teaspoon 3 times a day).

(ii) Onion is also good for tooth trouble. Chewing raw onion for three minutes is sufficient to kill all the germs in the mouth. Toothache is relieved by keeping a piece of onion on the affected tooth or gum.

(iii) Onion is proved to be an effective food item in preventing heart-attack. As per research, it contains essential oil, allylpropyl disulphide, catechol, proto-catechuic acid, thiopropionaldehyde, thiocyanate, calcium, iron, phosphorus and vitamins which keep check on heart troubles by correcting thrombosis and reducing blood cholesterol. (One should take 100 gms. of onion per day.)

(iv) Onion is a powerful aphrodisiac. It increases libido and strengthens the reproductory organs (two tablespoons, white onion juice, two tablespoons honey and one tablespoon dark juice mixed together and taken 3 times a day).

(v) Onion is used in skin diseases and stimulates the circulation of blood in the mucous membrane. Warts are dissolved by rubbing with onion pieces. Roasted onion is valued as a perfect remedy from ancient times for bruises and wounds. It is also used in the form of poultices in slight dislocation of joints etc.

(vi) Onion juice when dropped in ear stops ringing sound in the ears. Dropped hot in the ear, it relieves ear-ache.

(vii) Onion is a proven remedy in cholera. A paste of 30 gms of onion and seven black peppers and sugar to taste should be given in cholera. It immediately controls restlessness, thirst and vomiting.

(viii) Onions are good for urinary problems. For burning sensation in urine, 6 gms of onion should be boiled in half litre water which is reduced to further half quantity on fire. It is then cooled and given to patients. Onion rubbed in water and mixed with sugar to taste is useful in urine retention.

(ix) Onion is useful in bleeding piles. Method given for urine retention is also useful here. Onion rubbed with sugar water should be taken twice daily.

(x) It allays several types of hysterical attacks and when rubbed into the skin, it encourages hair growth.

(xi) It gets rid of freckles and soothes the pain of insect stings.

(xii) When applied to the skin it repels mosquitoes and it aids dissolving scar formation on wounds.

Potato (Aalu)

Botanical Name : *Solanum tuberosum*
Family Name : Solanaceae
Hindi Name : Aalu
Sanskrit Name : Golakandah
English Name : Potato

Description

Potato is the most popular and all-time useful vegetable in the world. It is an annual plant with underground swollen, stem tubers.

Distribution

Originally, it is native of South Ameria and was introduced in Europe later on. At one time it was considered poisonous but later on accepted as a food item and a substitute for wheat in food scarcity.

Parts Used

Leaves, stem.

Properties

Antispasmodic, antiphlogistic, antacid.

Forms of Use

Decoction, fluid extract, ointment.

Food Value

Potato is a nutritive vegetable in which main compound is starch but there is protein of high biological value. It contains good amount of alkaline salts. It is rich in soda, potash and vitamins A and B.

Potato analysis gives the following composition (per 100 grams of edible part):

Moisture	75%
Protein	1.6%

Fat	0.1%
Minerals	0.6%
Fibre	0.4%
Carbohydrates	22.6%
Calcium	10 mg
Phosphorus	40 mg
Iron	0.7 mg
Vitamin C	17 mg
Calorific Value	97

Medicinal Uses

The leaves, green tubers and fruits are dangerously toxic because of their high solanine content. Apart from its culinary value, the white tuber has various medicinal qualities:

(i) It has soothing effect in eye irritations and can be used as a paste on skin irritants, sores and haemorrhoids.

(ii) The water in which potatoes have been boiled, can be used to clean silver and restore a shine to furniture & leather objects.

(iii) The juice of the plant is used by some people to relieve heartburn and water brash.

(iv) Roasted potatoes act as antacid.

(v) Emollient and cleansing face masks are also made from it to treat greasy or wrinkled skin.

Radish (Muli)

Botanical Name : *Raphnus sativus*
Family Name : Crucifarae
Hindi Name : Muli
Sanskrit Name : Mulaka
English Name : Radish

Description

Radish is the most commonly used vegetable, an annual herb having no stem or branches. It has only one root which is normally cylindrical white/red fleshy, succulent, 3 to 7 cm thick and 10 to 20 cm long. It has a pungent flavour. There are many varieties of radish but familiar ones are white & red.

Distribution

It has its origin in Western Asia. It was cultivated in Egypt, Greece & Rome but now its cultivation is spread all over the world — America, Africa, Malaysia, Indonesia, India, China and other countries.

Parts Used

Root, leaves, seeds.

Properties

Diuretic, laxative, liver tonic, anti-scorbutic, carminative, stimulant, lithnotriptic.

Food Value

Radish is one of the richest sources of iron, calcium and sodium among all the common vegetables. Its leaves are used more as food item than roots. To derive all the benefits, eat raw vegetables. Cooking destroys nutritional contents and vitamins.

Analysis of radish and radish leaves gives the following composition (per 100 gms of edible part):

	Radish	Radish Leaves
Moisture	94.4%	90.8%
Protein	0.7%	3.8%
Fat	0.1%	0.4%
Minerals	0.6%	1.6%
Fibres	0.8%	1.0%
Carbohydrates	3.4%	2.4%
Calcium	35 mg	265 mg
Phosphorus	22 mg	60 mg
Iron	0.4 mg	3.6 mg
Vitamin C	15 mg	81 mg
Calorific Value	17	28

Small amount of vitamin B-Complex is present in both.

Medicinal Uses

(i) The leaves of radish are diuretic, antiscorbutic and laxative.

(ii) The juice and the fresh root are effective piles remedies. One should take 50 to 70 ml juice morning and evening for a week at least.

(iii) The juice is also of much value in dysuria and stranguary or severe urethral pain (doses—50 to 70 ml morning and evening). A cupful of radish leaf juice given once daily for 15 days, dissolves calculi in the urinary tract and cystitis — the swelling of bladder.

(iv) In chest complaints, a syrup prepared by mixing a teaspoonful of fresh radish juice with equal quantity of honey and small amount of rock salt given 3 times daily is highly useful in hoarseness, whooping cough, bronchial disorders.

(v) In jaundice, leaves of radish bring about miraculous relief. 500 ml juice should be obtained, glucose & lemon juice is also added and taken daily in divided doses.

(vi) In leucoderma, a paste of seeds in vinegar is applied on the white spots.

Soyabean (Bhat)

Botanical Name : *Glycine max mer*

Family Name : Leguminosae

Hindi Name : Bhat

Sanskrit Name : Garikulay

English Name : Soyabean

Distribution

The name Soya is of Chinese origin — Shu or Sou. At one time, Soya and honey were considered holy food. It has its first reference in a Chinese book of King Shennung of China (2838 BC). It is now a very famous crop all over the world.

Parts Used

Seed.

Properties

Nutritive, anti-diabetic, anti-eczema, anti-constipation, proteinous, provides amino-acids.

Forms of Use

Oil and seed as vegetable.

Food Value

Soyabean possesses high food value, containing protein, vitamins, minerals etc. Besides, it also has vitamins B_1, B_2, B_6, biotin, folic acid, pantothenic acid and X-tocopherol.

Soyabean analysis gives the following composition (per 100 gms):

Moisture	8%
Protein	43%
Fat	20%
Fibre	3.7%
Minerals	4.6%
Carbohydrates	21%

Calcium	240 mg
Phosphorus	690 mg
Iron	11.5 mg
Vitamin B-Complex and Vitamin E	
Calorific Value	43

Medicinal Uses

(i) Soyabean-milk is very useful in the treatment of several ailments. This milk is prepared by soaking beans overnight in water, removing their skin and grinding them to a fine paste. After that water is added three times to the paste and is boiled and filtered, and after adding sugar, it is used. It is just like natural milk.

(ii) It is also beneficial to diabetics as it contains very little amount of starch.

(iii) It is very useful in anaemic conditions as it contains enough iron.

(iv) Soyabean is regarded as a valuable food remedy in eczema and other skin diseases.

(v) Soyabean protein is complete in itself as it contains all the essential amino acids.

Spinach (Palak)

Botanical Name	: *Spinacia olerecea*
Family Name	: Chinopodi-aceae
Hindi Name	: Palak
Sanskrit Name	: Palankya
English Name	: Spinach

Description

Spinach is a leafy vegetable having broad deep green leaves. It is rated high in leafy vegetables, full of nutrition. This vegetable is a cool season annual crop which matures quickly.

Distribution

It was originated in Arabia. It was cultivated 2000 years ago in Persia and from there it spread to Spain (its name derived from a Spanish word). It is cultivated in India on a large scale.

Parts Used

Leaves.

Properties

Diuretic, demulcent, soothing, refrigerant, mild laxative, anti-anaemic, ophthalmic, anti-inflammatory.

Forms of Use

As vegetable, soup, juice & infusion.

Food Value

The chemical constituents of spinach are essential amino acids, iron, vitamin A and folic acid. It is one of the cheapest vegetables which supplies the same amount of protein as one gets from the same quantity of meat, fish, eggs and chicken.

Spinach analysis gives the following composition:

Moisture	92.1%
Protein	2.0%

Fat	0.7%
Minerals	1.7%
Fibre	0.6%
Carbohydrates	2.9%
Calcium	75 mg
Phosphorus	20 mg
Iron	11 mg
Vitamin C	30 mg
Small amount of Vitamin B-Complex	
Calorific Value	17

Medicinal Uses

(i) Spinach leaves are diuretic and mild laxative.

(ii) Spinach juice cleans the digestive tract by removing the collected waste product. It nourishes the intestines and tones up their movements. It is, therefore, an excellent food remedy for constipation.

(iii) Spinach is a source of high grade iron & contributes in the formation of blood. So, it is very useful in anaemia.

(iv) Spinach is a good source of calcium and other alkaline elements essential to keep tissues clean and retain blood alkalinity. So, it is an antacid too.

(v) Spinach also takes care of our eyes as it contains vitamin A in good amount. Therefore, it helps in controlling night blindness and other eye problems.

(vi) Spinach juice provides strength to the gums and helps in preventing and curing dental cavities. Chewing raw spinach leaves cures pyorrhoea. A mixture of carrot and spinach juice taken early in the morning cures bleeding and ulcerated gums.

(vii) Spinach is a rich source of folic acid and useful during pregnancy and lactation. Regular use of spinach during pregnancy helps prevent deficiency of folic acid, lack of which may cause abortion, shortness of breath, loss of weight and diarrhoea. It also increases production of milk during lactation.

(viii) Spinach juice, when taken with coconut water twice a day, works as a diuretic due to the combined action of both nitrates and potassium. It is useful in cystitis, nephritis and scanty urination caused due to dehydration.

(ix) Spinach leaves plus two teaspoonfuls fenugreek seeds containing a pinch of ammonium chloride and honey when infused, prove to be an effective expectorant tonic for bronchitis, TB, asthma and dry cough. Doses are 30 ml, three times daily.

Note: As it contains oxalic acid which is insoluble in stomach and intestine fluid, it is harmful in gravels, gout and liver disease. Therefore, it should not be used by those suffering from these diseases.

Tomato (Tamatar)

Botanical Name	: *Lycopersicon esculentum*
Family Name	: Solanaceae
Hindi Name	: Tamatar
Sanskrit Name	: Raktamaci
English Name	: Tomato

Description

Tomato is a worldwide popular vegetable. It is a shortlived perennial annual plant with vigorous tap root, extensive fibrous roots, solid, hairy stems and spirally arranged, mainly oval leaves. The fruit is a fleshy, round or lobed, smooth, red, yellow with flat seeds. It has now hundreds of varieties. Tomato is a native of South America from where it was brought to Europe. Now it is a popular vegetable and is available in the market worldwide. It is grown everywhere in America, Africa, India, China and holds second place after potato among vegetables.

Parts Used

Fruit & leaves.

Properties

Deobstruent, stimulant, anti-scorbutic, diuretic, anti-cancer, ophthalmic.

Food Value

Nearly 100 years back, tomato was considered poisonous. It was known as acid-forming food which might increase blood & tissue acidity. So, persons having acidity, gout, rheumatism & arthritis should avoid its use. But as per latest studies in nutritional chemistry, these ideas are baseless.

Tomato analysis (per 100 gms edible part) proves that it is full of nutritional and health giving qualities:

Moisture	91.1%
Protein	0.9%

Fat	0.2%
Minerals	0.5%
Fibre	0.8%
Carbohydrate	3.4%
Calcium	50 mg
Phosphorus	20 mg
Iron	0.4 mg
Vitamin C	30 mg
Small amount of Vitamin B-Complex	
Calorific Value	20

Medicinal Uses

(i) Tomato is a powerful deobstruent, removes diseased particles and opens natural channels of the body. It is a gentle, natural stimulant for kidneys and helps to wash away the toxins which cause diseases and contaminate our system.

(ii) Raw tomato juice is very popular and widely used. It has an alkaline reaction in our body and is highly nutritious containing good amount of vitamin C that increases on ripening.

(iii) Acids of tomato are malic, citric and oxalic. These acids combine with sodium or potassium to form sod malate, citrate and oxilate. After oxidation in our body, they give alkaline reaction products in the form of carbonates of sodium and potassium. This increases alkalinity in our body, not acidity as thought earlier. So, it is an antacid.

(iv) It is said to be very effective in controlling the percentage of sugar in the urine of diabetic patients. It has low carbohydrate content and is a good food for diabetics.

(v) Tomatoes are highly useful in the treatment of obesity. One or two ripe tomatoes taken early morning without breakfast is considered a safe method to reduce weight. Besides it provides basic nutrients & vitamin C.

(vi) Tomato is a rich source of vitamin A. So, it is a dependable preventive remedy against night blindness & other eye diseases. Tomato leaves are useful in optic nerve and eye weakness. Doses—a handful of fresh leaves of tomato kept for 15 minutes in a cup containing soft hot water. The water is decanted and a teaspoonful, three times before meals/breakfast daily is useful.

(vii) Eating a tomato early in the morning prevents formation of urinary calculi/stone as it has sufficient quantity of acids & vitamins A and C. It is proved that lack of these vitamins invites recurrent UTI and it causes calculi/stone formation. Tomato controls the acid value of urine to 5.5 or less, thereby reducing the chances of infection by increasing the acidity of the urine.

(viii) For respiratory disorders, a glassful of fresh tomato juice mixed with honey, a pinch of powdered cardamom seeds, taken after swallowing three peeled garlic cloves every night before going to bed is highly beneficial in the treatment of tuberculosis and other lung infections. It increases the body's resistance and prevents drug resistance and the relapse which is common in TB. In asthmatics, it reduces the congestion in the bronchioles and checks the hyper-secretion of mucus and reduces spasms.

(ix) Eating tomatoes regularly gives protection against cancer as it contains a compound lycopene, a vitamin-like compound that interferes with molecules that cause DNA damage that lead to prostate cancer. As per Journal of National Cancer Institute, the more tomatoes men eat, the less likely they are to get the disease. So, you could be protecting yourself against prostate cancer with every tomato you consume.

Vegetable Juices

The juices extracted from fresh raw vegetables are highly nutritious as they give all the cells and tissues of the body with the elements and nutritine enzymes they are in need. It is true that the body can derive these elements from whole vegetables. But the fresh juices can provide them in the manner in which they can be most easily digested and assimilated. A vitamin and mineral deficiency can thus be made much more quickly by drinking fresh juices than by eating raw vegetable as such.

Practically all vegetables make good juices, but some are bitter. The bitterest one is of bitter gourd (Karela), but it is wonderful for diabetes. However, vegetable juices can be divided into three main types:

(i) Juices from vegetable fruits—Tomatoes & cucumber
(ii) Juices from green-leafy vegetables—Cabbage & spinach
(iii) Juices from root vegetables—Carrot & radish

In most cases it is desirable to use juice individually and seperately. In no case more than three juices should be included in any one mixture. The broad rules applicable to combination of vegetable juices are that juices from vegetable fruits may be combined with those of the green-leafy vegetables but not juices of root vegetables. Juices of green-leafy vegetables may be combined with those of the root vegetables.

Vegetable juices soothe jaded nerves and gently carry away toxic matter and accumulated waste products. **They are best taken at least half an hour or more after meals. They should not be taken before meals or near the same time as fruit juices.** Many common ailments respond favourably to raw vegetable juices but avoid drinking juices kept at room temperature. Always drink fresh juices or pasteurized or refrigerated ones.

Doses of vegetable juice differ with age. An adult may take one full glass juice whereas children and infants half and quarter glass (in divided doses) respectively per day during day time *i.e.* after breakfast and after lunch (two times).

As far as their effects are concerned, raw juices are found to be very rejuvenating and nutritive and no side effect is noticed during juice therapy which normally goes on upto 15 to 30 days. In some cases its use varies as per disease, for example, in jaundice, juices of lemon, raddish, pomegranate, bitter gourd are given upto one month or till symptoms disappear and patient recovers a bit. Just for the sake of good health, vegetable and fruit juices can be drunk for a month or more, e.g. orange, mousambi, cabbage, lemon juices. But those juices containing pretty good amount of beta-carotene e.g. carrot juice, should not be taken beyond one month as it contains beta-carotene which breaks into vitamin A in our stomach. One should know that one unit of beta-carotene gives two units of vitamin A which accumulates in our liver and may be toxic if deposited in excess amount. Vitamin A is an anti-oxidant and thus free radical destroyer which causes various diseases and also strengthens our eyesight and mucus membrane but its long course use is not recommended.

Every kind of therapy—natural or synthetic juice is not advised on empty stomach barring exception. So, juices could not be taken on an empty stomach. Rather they should be taken just before the meals or half or an hour after meals/breakfast.

Juice of beetroot is a potent liver cleanser. It helps to purify the blood and it removes toxins. When taken alongwith carrot juice, it also helps to promote normal bleeding during menses. It corrects an irregular cycle.

Raw beet juice helps promote normal bowel movements and prevents constipation. It also helps to strengthen the blood vessels. It helps to improve blood circulation, removes clots and also helps to reduce cholesterol.

For making good juice, you could combine one beetroot with two carrots and one tomato and push it through a juicer. You could add some boiled and cold water if the juice is too thick.

Juice of radish is an excellent remedy for thinning down mucus, clearing sinuses, blocked nose, mucus related migraine etc. Raw radish can be grated or chopped and chewed. Its juice helps thin down mucus. It also helps to reduce gas formation and indigestion. Some people have a low level of stomach acids and get flatulence (gas) on consuming non-vegetarian foods.

Radish helps to reduce phlegm and cures sore throat due to phlegm. Radish has a cooling thermal nature.

In the summer season, some people exhibit heat signs like nose bleeds or headaches or rash all over the body. Radish juice helps to correct such disorders. Its juice helps in detoxification and cleanses the body.

If one wants to reduce mucus, eat at least 2-3 fresh radish daily. You can even extract its juice and take it by mixing it in a half cup water 3 times a day (one tablespoon juice in half cup boiled cool water).

The juice of watermelon has a cooling effect on the body. It is a natural diuretic. It helps to reduce oedema (water retention) and treat urinary tract infection (UTI). It also helps to correct constipation. It is high in potassium and low in sodium. Therefore, it is highly beneficial in reducing blood pressure. The seeds of watermelon can be chewed. They help eliminate constipation. They are rich in iron and benefit those who are anaemic. It is also very useful in treating depression & excess thirst.

One full glass juice is to be consumed daily by people having the above problems. However, those who are thin, weak and have "wind" problems, should not take it. Those suffering from bladder problems and cannot control urination, should avoid it.

Moreover, juices of seasonal fruits and vegetables may be taken throughout the season of that particular fruit or vegetable and they will do more good than harm even if they are used for quite long period especially when there is inflammation in the intestines.

It should be noted that while consuming the fruits & vegetable foods for their therapeutic benefits, you should also make appropriate overall dietary and lifestyle changes in order to get their maximum healing benefits.

Zinc: A Potential Health Metal

Among the various trace elements, iodine, iron, zinc, copper, selenium, chromium, manganese and fluorides are considered important for human health.

Role of iodine in thyroid metabolism and iron in haemoglobin synthesis has been known for almost one hundred years.

The inorganic elements have many functions: as component of bones, teeth, as electrolytes in maintaining water balance in the vascular system and tissues and in the prosthetic groups of enzymes among others.

The essentiality of zinc for humans was recognized only 30 years ago. Its role in growth development, neurosensory functions, immunity, wound healing and hormonal functions has now been well established.

Zinc (Zn: at. no. 30; at. wt. 65.38) is bluish white, almost silvery metal, occurring in group II-B of the Periodic Table, along with cadmium and mercury.

Like vitamins, trace elements are also needed to bring about various body's functions.

There are approximately 200 enzymes known to require zinc as part of their prosthetic groups for various functions and there are 500 zinc containing peptides in gene representation of diverse proteins. These include alcohol dehydrogenase, carbonic anhydrase, DNA and RNA polymerases and carboxypeptidase. Zinc is found in high concentration in the prostrate gland, sperm cells and the eyes, where it presumably plays important but still unknown functions.

A broad spectrum of medical conditions can be associated with nutritional zinc deficiency. These vary in severity depending upon the degree of the deficiency which includes stunted growth, foetal abnormalities, anorexia, hyprogonadism, infertility, white flacks on the fingernails, night blindness, alopecia, mood-alteration, loss of libido, impotence, hair growth arrest, anaemia, low serum albumin, retarded development of the reproductive system and acrodermatitis enteropathica (a genetic disorder due to zinc metabolism in humans). An unusual and interesting feature of zinc deficiency in rare individuals is an alteration in taste and smell perception. Some smells are enormously distorted, so that normal food or cooking smell perceives as foul and disgusting leading to refusal of food and consequent weight loss. Phytic acid (present in breads made from partially refinded flour) may prevent absorption of zinc from the intestine as it binds zinc (Zn^{++}) very tightly.

As said, zinc is essential component of enzymes present in many NAD and NADP linked dehydrogenoses, enzymes that promote the transfers of hydride ions from substrate molecules to the Co-enzymes NAD+ and NADP+ e.g. the NAD requiring enzyme alcohol dehydrogenase of the liver, which catalyses dehydrogenation of ethanol to yield acetaldehyde, contains two atoms of zinc (Zn^{++}), which appear to bind the NAD+ and NADP+ co-enzyme to the active site of the enzyme.

Zn^{++} is also an essential component of DNA and RNA Polymerase and thus participates in important enzymatic reactions involved in the replication and transcription of genetic information (zinc is also required for cell replication). Zinc (Zn^{++}) is also present in carbonic anhydrase, which catalyses the hydration of carbon dioxide into carbonic acid and in the proteolytic enzyme, carboxy-peptidase secreted into small intestine. The hormone insulin is also stored as a zinc complex.

I would suggest double dosage of zinc in diabetes than in normal individuals. Its concentration in tastes and prostrate and its effect on the maturation of spermatozoa affects the essentiality of this element in continuing the species (testicular, prostrate abnormalities and impotency may be due to the imbalance of zinc concentration in the organ).

Zinc is carried to blood, firmly bouned to metallo-proteins loosely bound to albumins and in erythrocytes and leukocytes. A number of human diseases are associated with lowered blood zinc. Excretion largely via pancreatic juice into the intestine, much dietary Zn is unabsorbed, little appears in the urine (300 mg/day approx. against apparent intake of 10-15 mg) unless proteinuria, cirrhosis of the liver of Zn hepatic porphyria are present when considerably larger amounts may be excreted. Actually, Zn itself is not considered an important constituent of the urine but it is known to be an important constituent of several enzyme systems which have role in the urinary system—changes make it noteworthy. It has been shown that the levels of these enzymes in the urine change during a number of pathalogical processes, notably those involving neoplastic changes in the renal tissues. So by estimating the Zn concentration in urine, we can find useful result pertaining to neoplastic diseases.

A published study says that giving zinc to malnourished babies and toddlers cuts the incidence of pneumonia by 41 percent and of diarrhoea by as much as 25 percent. Pneumonia and diarrhoeal diseases are the two most important causes of child mortality in the developing countries. So, the potential of zinc is enormous.

UNICEF is supporting several zinc studies and developing a multi vitamin containing zinc for use in poor countries. Zinc performs very important functions in the body in promoting growth and fighting infections that are caused by the ultimate consequence of its deficiency and result in death.

It is reported that zinc deficiency is often found along with iron deficiency in babies recently weaned from breast milk, because many inexpensive porridges used to feed them are poor in nutrients. But zinc levels are difficult to measure in humans, and nutritionists have only slowly recognized its critical role in human growth and immunity.

In the past few years, zinc has become a hot research topic showing that zinc can reduce illness caused by malaria, another major global killer. Zinc, like iron, usually must be taken daily and its requirement is more in third world countries.

The body supply of Zn, except that in the bones and hair, is in a state of constant movement as expected for such an important element. More rapid turnover occurs in pancreas, liver, kidney and spleen, less rapid in nucleoproteins, RBC and testes. A regular intake of Zinc is essential because unlike iron, there are no functional body stores of zinc for utilization. So, at least 15 mg/day of Zn is required by pregnant women, but lactating women require more. Zn is abundant in meat, eggs, sea food, milk and liver but rather low in fruits and green vegetables.

Zn salts are toxic only in large doses, the reported cases of poisoning being probably caused by contaminating cadmium. They are of pharmacological and therapeutic values, most of which are antiseptics, astringent, irritant, emetic and toxic.

Zinc preparations are locally used in alcohol or watery solutions, as washers for mouth, eyes, ears wounds and ulcers. They are used for the destruction of various abnormal tissues. Zn is used in medicine in combination with other therapeutic agents or in their preparations.

Zinc lozenges may shorten the duration of the common cold.

Five of the ten previous studies on the effectiveness of zinc lozenges in reducing duration of the common cold said that they work and the rest five said they don't. Researchers in Michigan attempted to resolve the issue. They randomly divided 50 people with early cold symptoms into two groups, who received either 12.8 milligram zinc acetate lozenges or sham pills every two to three hours while awake. The patients then rated the severity of their symptoms, such as sore throat, congestion, cough and running nose, in the following days. The researchers also looked into the possible effects of zinc on the level of cytokines, immune system molecules that may play a role in cold symptoms. Most symptoms, especially coughs, disappeared much faster for patients taking zinc, while the patients taking the sham pills reported symptoms for 4-5 days only. The researchers, however, did not find a significant difference in cytokine levels between the two groups.

The researchers attempted to verify the validity of the study also by asking the patients to guess whether they were taking the real zinc lozenge or the sham pill. This is also the first study on zinc lozenges to look into the possible effects of zinc on cytokine levels.

Twice as many patients taking zinc could correctly guess their group, compared with the patients taking the sham pills. This reduces the validity of the study. In addition, the results need to be verified in a larger number of people. Finally, the foundation that founded this study is affiliated to the company that holds a patent for zinc lozenges (Cold-Eeze).

There is still a great deal of controversy about the use of zinc acetate lozenges for cold symptoms. This study suggests, however, that people who take them within the first 24 hours of symptoms, may be able to shorten the duration of their cold by almost half.

Bibliography

1. Nadkarni, A.K., 1954. **Indian Materia Medica**, Bombay.
2. Kritikar and Basu, 1935. **Indian Medicinal Plants,** Allahabad.
3. Chopra and Nayyar, 1956. **Glossary of Ind. Med. Plants,** New Delhi.
4. Dartin, J.F., 1951. **Med. Plants of India & Pakistan,** Bombay.
5. Chopra and Verma, 1969. **Supl. to Gloss. of Ind. Med. Plants,** New Delhi.
6. Siddappa, G.S., 1986. **Food Preservation, 1986,** Indian Council of Agricultural Research (ICAR), New Delhi.
7. Huang, L., 1984. **Nat. Pdts. and Drug Res.,** Munksgard, Copenhagen.
8. Food and Nutrition, 1989. **Educational Planning Gp.,** Karol Bagh, New Delhi.
9. Chiej, R. 1984. **Medicinal Plants,** Mac Donald, London.
10. Satyavati and Raina, 1976. **Medicinal Plants,** CSIR, New Delhi.
11. **Wealth of India,** 1986. CSIR, New Delhi.
12. Ambasta, P. 1987. **Useful Plants of India,** CSIR, New Delhi.
13. Kapoor, L.D., 1990. **Handbook of Ayurvedic Medicinal Plants,** CRC, Florida.
14. Dahanukar, S., 1995. **Heal with Herbs,** CSIR, New Delhi.
15. Aman, Dr., 1985. **Medicinal Secret of Foods,** Indo-American Hospital, Mysore.
16. Verma, G.S., 1970. **Miracles of Indian Herbs,** Rasayan Pharmacy, New Delhi.

17. Singh, S.J., 1982. **Food Remedies,** NCCMR, Lucknow.

18. Walker, N.W., 1983. **Raw Vegetable Juices,** Jove Books, New York.

19. Powell, F.W., 1973. **Health from the Kitchen,** Health Science Press, England.

20. Mukherjee, K.R., 1983. **Protective Foods in Health and Disease,** Prakritik, Kolkata.

21. Hameed, A., 1988. **A Complete Book on Home Remedies,** Orient Paper Books, Delhi.

22. Dev, S., 1997. **Ethnotherapeutics and Modern Drug Development,** Curr. Sc., Bangalore.

Glossary

Abortifacient	...	An agent that promotes abortion.
Acne	...	A pimple-like eruption of the sebaceous glands of the skin, with accumulation of yellow secretion and black overgrowth of the horny layer of the skin.
After-pains	...	Painful contraction of the womb after child-birth.
Alopecia	...	A disease of the scalp resulting in complete or partial baldness.
Alternative	...	A drug which corrects disordered processes of nutrition and restores the normal function of an organ or of the system.
Amenorrhoea	...	Abnormal suppression of menses.
Anaemia	...	A deficiency of blood or of red blood-cells or of the red-colouring matter of the blood.
Anasarca	...	Dropsy.
Angina pectoris	...	A disease of the heart marked by severe constricting pains in the chest.
Anodyne	...	A drug that relieves pain.
Antacid	...	A drug which neutralises the acidity of the gastric juice.
Anthelmintic	...	A drug that kills intestinal worms.
Antihydrotic	...	A drug that cures periodic attacks.
Antiphlogistic	...	A drug which counteracts inflammation.
Antipyretic	...	A drug which reduces fever.

Antiscorbutic	...	A drug which prevents or cures scurvy.
Antispasmodic	...	A drug which counteracts spasmodic disorders.
Aperient	...	A mild purgative.
Aphrodisiac	...	A drug which promotes sexual desire.
Aphthae	...	Minute white ulcers on the tongue and in the mouth.
Apoplexy	...	Sudden loss of consciousness with some paralysis; stroke.
Ardor urine	...	A burning sensation while urinating.
Aromatic	...	A drug which is fragrant, spicy and mildly stimulant.
Ascaris	...	Intestinal parasitic roundworms.
Ascites	...	Abdominal dropsy.
Asthma	...	A chronic disorder of the bronchial tubes.
Astringent	...	A drug which arrests secretion or bleeding.
Atony	...	Lack of tension or muscular power.
Attenuent	...	An agent that dilutes fluids.
Bechic	...	A remedy for cough.
Bedsores	...	Ulceration on any part of the body exposed to pressure of bed-ridden patient.
Beriberi	...	A deficiency disease caused by lack of vitamin B_1.
Blenorrhoea	...	Excessive mucous discharge, particularly from the uro-genital organs.
Bright's disease	...	An acute or chronic disease of the kidneys.
Bronchitis	...	An inflammation of the air passages.
Bronchorrhoea	...	Excessive discharge from the bronchial mucous membrane.

Calculus	...	A hard and solid concretion formed in the body, especially in the urinary organs; it may be sand, gravel or stone, according to size.
Cancer	...	Any malignant growth.
Carbuncle	...	An acute suppurative inflammation of the skin and tissues under the skin, rapidly spreading around the original point of infection.
Caries	...	Decay of teeth.
Carminative	...	A drug which relieves flatulence.
Cathartic	...	A drug which induces active movement of the bowels.
Caustic	...	An agent that corrodes or destroys tissues.
Cellulitis	...	Inflammation of the cellular tissues under the skin.
Chancre	...	A syphilitic ulcer.
Chilblains	...	Congestion of the blood at the extremeties as a result of defective blood circulation caused by damp cold.
Cholagogue	...	A drug which promotes flow of bile.
Chorea	...	A disease, chiefly in children, marked by irregular, spasmodic and involuntary actions of the limbs and face; St. Vitus's dance.
Chylous urine	...	Urine with a white milky fluid in which fat globules are in suspension.
Colic	...	Pain due to spasmodic contraction of the abdomen.
Congestion	...	An abnormal collection of blood in the blood vessels of any organ or part of the body.
Conjunctivitis	...	Inflammation of the conjunctiva, the mucous membrane covering the eyeball and lining the eyelids.

Contusion ... An injury to the soft parts without breaking the skin.

Counterirritant ... An agent which induces a mild irritation or inflammation of the skin to relieve congestion of the deeper structures.

Croup ... A diseased condition of the larynx of children characterized by difficult and noisy breathing accompanied by a hoarse cough.

Cystitis ... Inflammation of the bladder.

Dandruff ... An inflamed condition of the scalp characterized by the presence of white scales in the hair due to the exfoliation of the horny cells of the scalp.

Delirium ... An extreme mental disturbance marked by excitement, restlessness and rapid succession of confused and unconnected ideas.

Demulcent ... An agent having a soothing effect on the skin and mucous membranes.

Deobstruent ... A drug that removes an obstruction to secretion or excretion by opening the natural passages or pores of the body.

Depilatory ... An agent that removes or destroys hair.

Diabetes ... A wasting disease of metabolism; in one form of the disease, abundant sugar is present continuously in the urine; in the other form, abundant sugar is not present but there is excessive discharge of urine which is of low specific gravity and pale in colour.

Diaphoretic ... A drug that induces copious perspiration.

Diphtheria ... An infectious disease of the throat and the air passage which become inflamed

		and swollen and are coated with a fibrinous exudate.
Discutient	...	A drug which disperses or absorbs a tumour or any coagulated fluid in the body.
Diuretic	...	A drug which increases the secretion and discharge of urine.
Dropsy	...	A disease marked by an excessive collection of a watery fluid in the tissues or cavities of the body.
Dysentery	...	An infectious disease, the chief symptoms of which are acute diarrhoea and discharge of mucus and blood.
Dysmenorrhoea	...	Unusually painful and difficult menstruation.
Dyspepsia	...	Indigestion.
Dysuria	...	Painful and difficult urination.
Eczema	...	A skin disease accompanied by swelling, redness and exudation of lymph.
Elephantiasis	...	A disease of the skin caused by a tiny worm and attended with hypertrophy of the affected parts.
Emetic	...	A drug which induces vomiting.
Emmenagogue	...	A drug which promotes menstruation or regulates the menstrual periods.
Emollient	...	A drug which allays irritation of the skin and alleviates swelling and pain.
Enteritis	...	Inflammation of the intestines.
Epilepsy	...	A chronic nervous disorder marked by attacks of unconsciousness or convulsions.
Escharotic	...	An agent capable of destroying tissues.
Excoriation	...	Removal of the skin by rubbing or chafling.

Expectorant	... A drug that promotes the removal of catarrhal matter and phlegm from the bronchial tubes.
Febrifuge	... An agent used for reducing fever.
Fistula	... An abnormal channel which connects one cavity of the body with another, or which opens out from a cavity to the surface of the body.
Flatulence	... A disorder in which there is an excessive collection of gas in the stomach.
Freckles	... Coloured spots on the exposed parts of the skin.
Galactagogue	... An agent that promotes secretion and flow of milk.
Gleet	... A chronic discharge from the urethra.
Glycosuria	... A diseased condition of the urine in which sugar is excreted.
Goitre	... A chronic enlargement of the thyroid gland.
Gonorrhoea	... An infectious venereal disease marked by an inflammatory discharge from the genital organs.
Gravel	... A collection of tiny stone-like particles of uric acid, calcium oxalate or phosphates in the organs of the urinary system.
Griping	... Sharp pain due to the presence of some irritating substance in the bowels.
Guinea-worm	... A very slender worm infecting human beings through drinking contaminated water; it gradually works its way into subcutaneous tissues.
Haemoptysis	... Spitting of blood from the lungs or bronchial tubes.

Haemoptysis	...	Spitting of blood from the lungs or bronchial tubes.
Haemorrhage	...	Bleeding, especially profuse, from any part of the body.
Heartburn	...	A burning feeling in the regions of the chest and stomach, generally due to indigestion.
Hemicrania	...	Migraine.
Hemiplegia	...	Paralysis of one side of the body.
Hepatic	...	Pertaining to the liver.
Hepatitis	...	Inflammation of the liver.
Hernia	...	Rupture; protrusion through its covering of any organ of the body.
Herpes	...	A deep-seated vesicular eruption causing neuralgic pains.
Hysteria	...	A disease in which a physically healthy patient has lost control over acts and feelings and suffers from imaginary ailments.
Indolent	...	Painless; inactive.
Induration	...	Area of hardened tissue.
Intermittent fever	...	Fever which is marked by intervals of normal temperature between periods of rise of temperature.
Itch	...	An infectious skin disease, caused by a mite, without specific lesions and marked by excessive itching; scabies.
Jaundice	...	A diseased condition in which there is a yellowish staining of the tissues and excretions with bile.
Lactagogue	...	Galactagogue.
Lactifuge	...	A drug that checks the secretion of milk.
Laryngitis	...	Inflammation of the larynx.

Leprosy	...	A chronic wasting disease caused by a germ; the disease generally results in mutilations and deformities.
Leucoderma	...	A condition of the skin in which there is loss of pigment wholly or partially.
Lithontriptic	...	A drug used for removing calculi or stones formed in the urinary system.
Lochia	...	The vaginal discharge following childbirth.
Lochiorrhoea	...	An excessive flow of lochia.
Malaria	...	A recurrent disease marked by bouts of shivering, sudden rise of temperature and general aching of the body; ague.
Mania	...	A mental disorder marked by dangerous excitement or insane or morbid craving.
Measles	...	An infectious febrile disease, chiefly of children, marked by a cold in the head, running of the eyes and nose and appearance of white tiny spots on the inner side of the cheek and of rashes all over the body.
Melancholia	...	A disorder of the mind marked by depression of spirits and mental sluggishness.
Menopause	...	Change of life.
Menorrhagia	...	Abnormally excessive menstruation.
Metrorrhagia	...	Bleeding from the womb.
Micturation	...	Urination
Migraine	...	Periodic attack of headache affecting one side of the head.
Mumps	...	An infectious disease marked by the inflammation of the glands near the ear.
Narcotic	...	A drug which induces deep sleep.
Nausea	...	A feeling that vomiting is about to take place.

Nephritis	...	Inflammation of the kidneys.
Neuralgia	...	Pain felt along a nerve.
Night-blindness	...	A disease in which the patient is incapable of seeing in the dark.
Ophthalmia	...	Conjunctivitis.
Orchitis	...	Inflammation of the testicles.
Otitis	...	Inflammation of the ear.
Otorrhoea	...	A purulent discharge from the ear.
Ovaritis	...	Inflammation of the ovaries.
Paralysis	...	A disease in which there is loss of power of voluntary movement in any part of the body.
Pectoral	...	A drug to cure disorders of the chest.
Pharyngitis	...	Inflammation of the pharynx.
Phythisis	...	Consumption; tuberculosis of the lungs.
Piles	...	An inflamed condition of the veins in the rectal region.
Pityriasis	...	A scaly skin disease.
Pleurisy	...	Inflammation of the membrane enclosing the lungs.
Pneumonia	...	Inflammation of the lungs.
Prolapse	...	The falling downward of an organ of the body from its normal position.
Prophylactic	...	An agent that prevents disease.
Prurigo	...	A chronic skin disease marked by the eruption of small, rounded, reddish pimples.
Psoriasis	...	A common chronic inflammation of the skin, marked by rounded reddened patches which are covered with dry silvery scales.

Puerperium	...	The period between childbirth and the return of the womb to its normal condition.
Pulmonary	...	Pertaining to the lungs.
Pyorrhoea	...	A disease marked by purulent discharge from the gums.
Refrigerant	...	A drug which relieves feverishness or produces a feeling of coolness.
Remittent fever	...	Fever in which the temperature fluctuates considerably, but does not drop to the normal.
Rheumatism	...	An indefinite term used for pains in the muscles, joints and certain tissues.
Ringworm	...	A parasitic skin disease usually marked by red, scaly, circular patches.
Roundworm	...	A pinkish, intestinal, parasitic worm resembling the common earthworm.
Rubefacient	...	A mild counter-irritant.
Scabies	...	An itching skin disease caused by a mite.
Sciatica	...	An inflammation of the sciatic nerve at the back of the thigh.
Scorbutic	...	Suffering from scurvy.
Scrofula	...	A disease of the lymphatic gland, often of the neck.
Scurvy	...	A deficiency disease due to lack of vitamin C.
Sedative	...	A drug which promotes salivation.
Sinus	...	Medically the term means a suppurating tract that has not healed up.
Soporific	...	A drug that induces sleep.
Sprue	...	Chronic inflammation of the digestive tract, marked by indigestion and morning diarrhoea.

Stomatitis	...	Inflammation of the mouth.
Strangury	...	Painful and drop by drop discharge of urine.
Stomachic	...	A drug that strengthens the stomach and promotes its action.
Styptic	...	An agent which checks bleeding.
Syphilis	...	A chronic venereal disease.
Tenesmus	...	Involuntary, painful, spasmodic and frequent straining to evacuate the bowel.
Tetanus	...	An infectious disease, marked by painful contraction in the muscles.
Threadworm	...	A very small thin worm commonly infecting children; its habitat is the large intestine.
Tonsilitis	...	Inflammation of the tonsils.
Tympanites	...	Distention of the abdomen due to the collection of gas.
Typhoid fever	...	An acute infectious disease characterized by ulceration of the intestines, eruption of rose-coloured spots, and a typical course of temperature.
Typhus fever	...	An acute contagious and infectious disease marked by high temperature, acute depression and eruptions.
Ulcer	...	An open sore on the skin.
Urethritis	...	Inflammation of the urethra, the canal which extends from the bladder and discharges the urine.
Urticaria	...	An allergic disease of systemic origin marked by painful and itching elevations of the skin.
Vermifuge	...	A drug which expels intestinal worms.

Vertigo	...	Dizziness.
Vesicant	...	An agent that produces a blister.
Vulnerary	...	A drug which promotes healing of wounds.
Wart	...	A hypertrophy of or growth on the skin.
Whipworm	...	A common parasite in men; the worm has a thick body and a slender neck; it resembles a whip.
Whitlow	...	A septic inflammation of the tissues surrounding the nail or of the bone of the distal joint of a finger or toe.
Whooping cough	...	An acute infectious disease characterized by peculiar spasmodic attacks of coughing.

Books on General Health & Remedies

Postage:
Rs. 20/- on
each book.

Every
subsequent book:
Rs. 5/- extra.

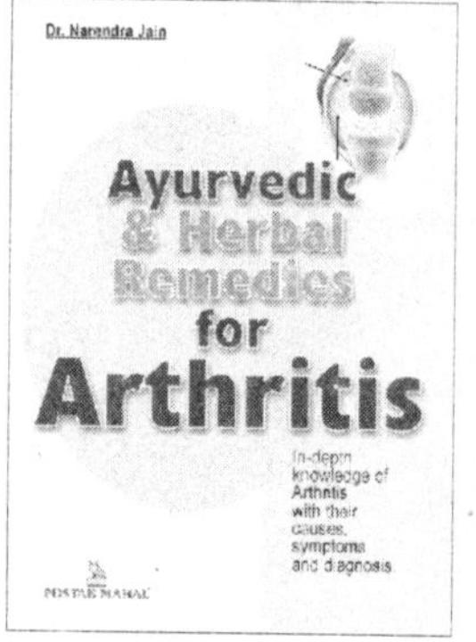